MATT AND TOM OLDFIELD

CLASSIC
FOOTBALL HEROES

BECKHAM

**FROM THE PLAYGROUND
TO THE PITCH**

DINO

First published by Dino Books in 2018,
an imprint of Bonnier Books UK,
The Plaza,
535 Kings Road,
London SW10 0SZ

🐦 @dinobooks
🐦 @footieheroesbks
www.heroesfootball.com
www.bonnierbooks.co.uk

Text © Matt Oldfield 2018

Design and typesetting by www.envydesign.co.uk

Paperback ISBN: 978 1 78606 921 4
E-book ISBN: 978 1 78606 941 2

British Library Cataloguing-in-Publication Data:
A catalogue record for this book is available from the British Library.

Printed and bound in Great Britain by Clays Ltd, Elcograf S.p.A.

5 7 9 10 8 6 4

MIX
Paper from
responsible sources
FSC® C018072

For Noah and Nico,
Southampton's future strikeforce

Matt Oldfield is an accomplished writer and the editor-in-chief of football review site *Of Pitch & Page*. Tom Oldfield is a freelance sports writer and the author of biographies on Cristiano Ronaldo, Arsène Wenger and Rafael Nadal.

Cover illustration by Dan Leydon.
To learn more about Dan visit danleydon.com
To purchase his artwork visit etsy.com/shop/footynews
Or just follow him on Twitter @danleydon

TABLE OF CONTENTS

ACKNOWLEDGEMENTS

First of all, I'd like to thank John Blake Publishing –
and particularly my editor James Hodgkinson – for
giving me the opportunity to work on these books
and for supporting me throughout. Writing stories for
the next generation of football fans is both an honour
and a pleasure.

I wouldn't be doing this if it wasn't for Tom. I
owe him so much and I'm very grateful for his belief
in me as an author. I feel like Robin setting out on a
solo career after a great partnership with Batman. I
hope I do him (Tom, not Batman) justice with these
new books.

Next up, I want to thank my friends for keeping

7

me sane during long hours in front of the laptop.
Pang, Will, Mills, Doug, John, Charlie – the laughs
and the cups of coffee are always appreciated.

I've already thanked my brother but I'm also very
grateful to the rest of my family, especially Melissa,
Noah and of course Mum and Dad. To my parents, I
owe my biggest passions: football and books. They're
a real inspiration for everything I do.

Finally, I couldn't have done this without Iona's
encouragement and understanding during long,
work-filled weekends. Much love to you.

CHAPTER 1

ALWAYS A WINNER

18 May 2013 – Paris, France

This was it. After twenty amazing years, David's life as a professional footballer was about to end. He had always known that his final match would be emotional, but he was holding back the tears before the game had even kicked off.

'Am I doing the right thing?' David asked himself.

He was thirty-eight years old now and his tired body was telling him to stop. His head, however, was telling him to keep doing what he loved, and so were the PSG fans in the Parc des Princes stadium.

'Beckham, one more year please!' one of their banners read.

But no, he wanted to quit while he was still at the

top of his game, while he could still help his team.

During his career, David had played with so many superstars. He listed them in his head:

Eric Cantona, Ryan Giggs and Paul Scholes –
at Manchester United

Michael Owen, Steven Gerrard and Wayne
Rooney – with England

Ronaldo, Roberto Carlos, Zinedine Zidane
and Luís Figo – at Real Madrid

Landon Donovan and Robbie Keane –
at LA Galaxy

Paolo Maldini, Ronaldinho and Kaká –
at AC Milan

...and now Zlatan Ibrahimović at PSG. What a list! It was a great honour to be able to call them friends, as well as teammates. They had all inspired David to keep striving for improvement and perfection. Like them, he was always a winner.

'Are you ready, Becks?' Zlatan said, giving him a high-five.

'Ready as I'll ever be,' David smiled back, fixing the armband on his sleeve. The PSG manager, Carlo

Ancelotti, had made him the captain for the final home match of the season against Brest.

David's family was there watching in the Parc des Princes stadium, and the names of his children – Brooklyn, Romeo, Cruz and Harper – were stitched into his special white, red and blue Adidas boots. His children meant so much to him, and so did his wife, Victoria.

Next to their names were his shirt numbers – 7 for Manchester United and England, 23 for Real Madrid and LA Galaxy, and 32 for AC Milan and PSG.

And next to his shirt numbers was the Union Jack flag. No matter where David played – Spain, America, Italy or France – he was always proud to be English.

'Right, let's do this!' David shouted to his teammates.

PSG were 1–0 up after four minutes thanks to another Zlatan goal. It was party time for the Champions of France but what could David do to celebrate his big day? Could his remarkable right foot create one last bit of magic?

Ever since he was a young boy, David had worked so hard to make the most of his talent. He had an unusual technique for striking the ball, but hours of practice made perfect. When it came to long-range shots, long-range passes, free kicks and corners, he was the best in the business.

After thirty minutes, PSG won a corner. As David walked over to take it, he slowed down to enjoy the feeling of being so close to the fans. No matter what team he played for, the fans' noise and passion always left him buzzing. It had inspired him so many times over the years. David remembered his two late corners in the 1999 Champions League final, when Manchester United fought back to complete the Treble. What a night!

Football was never over until the final whistle blew – that's what his old Manchester United manager Sir Alex Ferguson had taught him. David chipped a teasing cross towards the penalty spot. It was another dangerous delivery, but could someone get on the end of it? His midfield partner Blaise Matuidi could. He hit it on the volley and scored. 2–0!

'Thanks, you're the best teammate ever!' he screamed.

David was pleased to get one last assist, but could he get one last goal? He hadn't yet scored for PSG but there was still time to say goodbye in style.

When his team won a free kick, the fans urged him to take it. But David was a team player, not a greedy player. It was Zlatan's turn to strike it. 'Just do me proud!' David told him.

'Yes, captain.' The Swedish striker bent the ball around the wall and into the top corner. 3–0!

'Beckham, eat your heart out!' Zlatan laughed as they celebrated together.

With ten minutes to go, it was finally time for David to leave the field for good. He had given his all, just like always. He took a deep breath and tried not to cry, but it was no use. As his teammates came over to hug him one by one, tears filled his eyes. By the time he reached his manager Ancelotti on the touchline, the tears were streaming down his face.

'It's a historic moment,' a voice boomed around the stadium. 'DAVID...'

'BECKHAM!' the fans roared.

'*Merci*, David!' they chanted.

David Beckham! David Beckham! David Beckham!

After the match, David walked around the pitch, clapping to the crowd. He had only been at PSG for five months, but it really felt like home. His teammates threw him high into the air, once, twice and a third time for luck.

'We'll miss you, Becks!' they shouted.

David was going to miss them too. He was going to miss playing football so much. Ever since his first kick, football had been his focus, his life. It was hard to believe that his incredible playing career was over. His adventure had taken him from London to Paris, via Manchester, Madrid, Los Angeles, Milan and so many other exciting places.

Through hard work and dedication, he had risen through the ranks at his beloved Manchester United to become one of the most famous footballers on the planet. Although his cabinet was already full to the brim, David had one last trophy to collect – the Ligue 1 title.

'I want to say thank you to everybody in Paris - to my teammates, to the staff, to the fans,' he spoke into the microphone, wearing an England flag like a cape. 'It's been very special to finish my career here. I feel I've achieved everything I could. I wanted to go out as a champion and I have.'

At club level, David had won the league in four different countries – England, Spain, the USA, and now France. He was the only Englishman to ever achieve that and he had also won the Champions League and the FA Cup.

At international level, David hadn't won any trophies but there was still so much to be proud of. He had won 115 caps for his country, 58 as captain. He had played at three World Cups, scoring in each of them.

No, he hadn't quite managed to lead the Three Lions to glory, but David had bounced back from national villain in 1998 to become a national hero again in 2001, thanks to a last-minute free kick against Greece that took England to the 2002 World Cup. The England fans would never forget that.

That was a goal that took real guts, one of David's greatest strengths – along with, of course, his remarkable right foot.

CHAPTER 2

MANCHESTER UNITED MAD

'What do you think, son?' Ted asked with a proud smile on his face. 'I think red really suits you!'

David giggled, threw his little arms up in the air, and ran around the room in circles.

'I think he agrees!' his mum Sandra laughed from behind the video camera.

Ted was a huge football fan. Although the Beckham family lived in London, he didn't support Tottenham or Arsenal, or Chelsea or West Ham. No, he was Manchester United mad, and he often travelled up to Old Trafford to watch his favourite team play.

When it came to his son's third birthday, Ted knew exactly what to buy him – his first Manchester United kit.

'You're never too young to become a Red Devil,' Ted told his wife. 'Plus, your father is trying to turn him into a Spurs fan and we can't have that!'

The shirt looked a little big on David, but he'd soon grow into it. Then, once he'd grown out of that one, he'd get another one, perhaps with his favourite player's name on the back. And soon, he'd be ready for his first trip to Old Trafford. Ted couldn't wait to take his son to his first match.

'You're going to love it there, son. It's the Theatre of Dreams!'

Ted still played football for a team called Kingfisher in the local league but once upon a time, he'd had trials with Leyton Orient. He was a big, tough striker but he never quite had the speed or skill to make it as a professional. Now, he hoped that maybe his football dream could become his son's football dream.

'He's going to be the next Bobby Charlton!' Ted told everyone confidently.

David's football journey had started as soon as he could walk. His dad dropped balls at his feet and then stood back and watched.

'Go on, kick!' Ted cheered lovingly, swinging his leg through the air to demonstrate.

When David picked the ball up with his hands instead, his dad didn't lose hope. 'Perhaps he'll be United's next goalkeeper!' he thought to himself.

Soon, however, David learnt to kick, and once he started kicking, he never stopped kicking. He was a natural. He kicked anything and everything in his path – footballs, tennis balls, stones, socks... even his sister Lynne's Care Bear toys.

'Mum!' Lynne cried out from the top of the stairs. 'David's doing it again!'

Now that he had his first Manchester United shirt, it was even harder to stop him kicking. He raced around the living room, wearing holes in the carpet. Luckily, he couldn't do too much damage with a small, soft ball.

'*Goooooooooooooooooooaaaaaaaaaaaaaaaalllllllllll lllllllllllllll!!!!!!!!!!!!!!!!!!!!*' David cheered.

'Okay, that's enough – you're going to make yourself dizzy!' Sandra warned him gently. 'Why doesn't Daddy take you out into the back garden for a bit of fresh air?'

'Good idea!' Ted replied happily.

It was a bright, sunny May afternoon and there was a ball out there waiting for them. Their kickabout started softly, but David's kicks were getting more and more powerful.

'That's it, son!' his dad cheered, urging him on. He could see it now, his son scoring at Old Trafford. 'Try kicking it even harder!'

'No, no, no – stop!' Sandra groaned loudly. She should have known better than to let them loose in her garden. Even from the back door, she could see the damage. Her beautiful flowerbeds were flattened and ruined.

David looked up at her with big, innocent eyes. 'Mummy, what's wrong? Do you want to play too? One day, I'll play for Man U!' he said proudly, pointing down at his muddy red shirt.

His mum's anger disappeared straight away. How could she argue with that?

'Sorry,' her husband said guiltily, picking up the football. 'We got a little carried away, didn't we, David? Come on son, we'll go and play in the park instead!'

CHAPTER 3

PRACTICE MAKES PERFECT

Chase Lane Park was just around the corner from their house. It was David's favourite place in the world, a football fantasy land. There were big, empty grass pitches with white line markings and real goal posts. What more could you want?

'Slow down!' Ted called out. He had to walk quickly just to keep up with his excited son.

At the beginning, David just dribbled past imaginary defenders and took shots against his dad. That was really fun but by the age of six, he was ready for something a little more serious.

'Dad, if I want to play for Manchester United one day, what do I need to do?' David asked with a focused look on his young face.

Ted smiled and clapped his hands. It was the question that he'd been hoping for. 'Well, son, let me show you!'

He kicked the ball high up into the air and told David to control it. 'Watch it carefully,' Ted said, 'all the way onto your boot!'

At first, the ball went everywhere, no matter how carefully David watched it. It bounced off his shin, it rolled off his boot, and sometimes it even missed his boot completely. But eventually, he managed to trap the ball nicely and pass it back to his dad. David was delighted. He thought his first lesson was over, but he thought wrong.

'Good, now try another ten,' Ted called out. 'Practice makes perfect!'

The next lesson was striking the ball. David thought he was already quite good at that, but it turned out he still had a lot to learn. His dad stood there, tall and wide, between David and the goal.

'Try to score!' Ted challenged him.

The only way to score was to bend the ball around

him. That took hours and hours of practice, but David kept going, even when his legs ached, and when night was falling around them.

'I can do this,' he told himself.

Sometimes, when things weren't going well, David wished his dad would just go in goal and let him shoot, like the other parents at Chase Lane Park. But most of the time, he was grateful for Ted's help. He couldn't make it all the way to Manchester United on his own.

David's striking technique was unique, but also very successful. He placed the ball down and took six steps back. As he ran up, he swung his left arm backwards and his right foot forwards to get maximum power. He kicked it with the side of his big toe to get extra curl and spin as it flew around his dad and into the net.

'Good, now try another ten,' Ted called out, again. 'Practice makes perfect!'

Even when his dad was away at work, David still went down to Chase Lane Park. It was where he always wanted to be. If there were other kids around, he asked to join in their games. David was usually quite a shy child, but football gave him the confidence to talk to the big boys. Some of them were double his age and most of them were double his skinny size.

'Sure! What's your name? Everyone, this is David. Neil, he's on your team now!'

David enjoyed testing his talent in proper matches, especially against bigger, stronger kids. Whenever he took a knock, he just got up and got on with the game, just like his dad had always taught him. If he got tackled, it meant that he needed to think faster.

'Look for the space,' he kept telling himself.

If he was on his own, David just practised his shots and passes. There was a small hut in the corner of Chase Lane Park, with wire covering the windows. He aimed for that wire again and again and each time he hit it, he moved a little bit further away. That way, his accuracy was improving all the time.

Most people would have found that boring and repetitive, but not David. Hours would fly by and he would still be having fun. His dad's words were always there in his head – 'Practice makes perfect'.

By the age of seven, David had a new favourite place. Wadham Lodge was the home of Kingfisher, his dad's team. It was no Old Trafford, but it was a better football fantasy land than Chase Lane Park. There were goal nets, changing rooms, dugouts and even floodlights.

'This place is amazing!' David marvelled out loud. 'One day, I'm going to play here.'

Whenever his dad would let him, he went along to training and they kicked a ball around on the pitch before and after the session. David loved watching all of the emotion and drama on display. Competitive football looked so exciting. By the end, he couldn't wait for his turn to play. Once everyone else had gone home, it was free-kick time. David placed the ball down outside the penalty area and stepped back to strike it.

'Right, I'll give you 50p for every time you hit the crossbar,' Ted challenged his son.

Challenge accepted and soon, challenge completed! Even as a young kid, David was earning money with his remarkable right foot.

CHAPTER 4

RIDGEWAY ROVERS

When David was eight, his dad stopped playing for Kingfisher. As much as Ted loved playing football, he couldn't go on forever. His creaking body wouldn't let him, so he focused on coaching instead, and coaching one youngster in particular.

'Taxi driver at your service,' Ted joked to David, pretending to bow.

By then, David was playing so much football that his parents could barely keep up. He was playing for Chase Lane Primary School and the Cubs, as well as all the friendly matches at Chase Lane Park and Wadham Lodge. If there was a game going on, David would be there as fast as his little legs could carry him.

'Don't you ever get bored?' his younger sister, Joanne, asked him. She liked following her brother around, but it was always just football, football and more football. It was so dull.

'No, never!' he replied as if it was the silliest question in the world. He couldn't get enough.

One day, Ted saw an advert in the local newspaper for a new boys' team called Ridgeway Rovers. They were holding trials around the corner in Chase Lane Park.

'What do you think?' he asked, showing it to his son.

'Let's go!' David said straight away.

Stuart Underwood was the manager of the Ridgeway Rovers. He knew that there were lots of talented young players in the neighbourhood and his dream was to bring them together and turn them into a really good team. As he laid out the cones and sorted the bibs, Stuart started to feel a little anxious.

What if no-one turned up?

Not a problem! There were already a few boys kicking a ball around with his son, Robert.

Okay, well what if all the kids turned out to be terrible?

Not a problem! With the right kind of coaching, Stuart would turn them into world-beaters.

'Welcome, everyone!' Stuart's voice boomed across the park. He was a big guy and some of the kids looked terrified as he loomed over them. 'Thanks for coming along this afternoon. Right, let's have some fun!'

David had lots of fun. He loved showing off his excellent ball control and passing range, especially on home soil at Chase Lane Park. All of those hours with his dad had prepared him well.

When he got a little over-confident, Stuart told him so. 'Keep it simple, kid. We're not Brazil – not yet, anyway!'

In his head, however, the Ridgeway Rovers manager was thinking, 'Wow, he's special!' The kid had great technique, but he also had a great attitude. Stuart could see that David was eager to learn and improve. 'That's it – lovely!' he said, encouragingly.

Even in that very first practice, David made lots of

new friends. Robert, Ryan, Steve, Jason, Micah, Chris – they were all good players and a good laugh too.

'Dad, please can I join?' David asked eagerly at the end.

When it came to football, Ted could never say no, and soon he was even one of Ridgeway's coaches.

'Don't expect an easy ride just because you're my son,' he warned.

David smiled. 'Dad, you've been coaching me all my life! Don't worry, I know what to expect. I'm ready to work twice as hard as the other boys.'

To get everyone up to speed, Ridgeway ran two training sessions a week. Stuart was firm but fair with his players. His rules were simple. If you didn't turn up for training, you didn't play at the weekend. If you weren't giving 110 per cent effort on the pitch, you were taken off.

'It's all about commitment,' their manager told them.

David's commitment was never in doubt. He was preparing himself to one day become a professional. He never stopped believing.

The hard work and team spirit soon paid off, as the Ridgeway Rovers took the local league by storm. After a couple of seasons, they were winning every trophy up for grabs.

'Boys, you're the best team that I could ever ask for,' Stuart told them proudly.

David loved every minute of it. He was Ridgeway's wing wizard, whipping in excellent crosses all game, every game. He swung his left arm backwards and his remarkable right foot forwards. Boom! He curled the ball into the box and straight onto Chris's head.

Goooooooooooooooooooooaaaaaaaaaaaaaaaaalllllllllllll llllllllllllll!!!!!!!!!!!!!!!!!!!!!

But the more goals David set up, the more tough tackles and crafty kicks came his way. As one of the smallest players on the pitch, it was the easiest way to keep him quiet.

'Arghhhhhh!' he cried out.

David always tried to get up and get on with the game, just like his dad had always taught him, but that wasn't always possible. Sometimes, the boy left the pitch in so much pain that he had to miss the next match. A week without football was the worst thing ever. What could he do to avoid the injuries?

'Sometimes, you've got to release the ball early,' Ted taught him in the park. 'Pass and move, pass and move. Defenders will find it harder to foul you if you've already passed it on to the next player!'

As ever, David listened carefully and learnt his lessons quickly. It was all part of his big plan – to become a professional footballer and make it all the way to Manchester United.

For now, however, he already had offers to train with four London clubs: West Ham, Wimbledon, Arsenal and Tottenham. In the end, David chose Tottenham.

'Just you wait until Grandad hears the news,' his mum said. 'He'll be so proud of you!'

David was proud of himself too. He had earned this amazing opportunity at a top English club. It was just a shame that it wasn't Manchester United. Even on his first day at Tottenham, he refused to hide his favourite team. He ignored his mum's advice and wore his red shirt to White Hart Lane.

'You do know you're at Spurs, right?' asked their brilliant young defender, Sol Campbell, during the warm-up.

David nodded. His grandad had bought him lots of Tottenham shirts when he was younger, but he would always be a Red Devil.

'You're either very brave or very stupid!' their skilful midfielder Nick Barmby added with a grin.

CHAPTER 5

MOVING TO MANCHESTER UNITED

Manchester United had a team of scouts spread out all over the country. Malcolm Fidgeon was their man in London and he had a very busy job. There was no way that he could watch every talented youngster in the city, but he gave it his best shot.

One day, Malcolm was at an Under-12s game between Redbridge and Waltham Forest. He had heard wonderful things about one of Waltham Forest's young players, a small winger with a remarkable right foot.

'Let's see what you've got, kid,' the scout muttered under his breath as the match kicked off.

Malcolm was ready to be disappointed. Manchester United were only looking for the very best players, kids with amazing talent *and* the right attitude. Time and time again, he saw one but not the other.

Sometimes, Malcolm found skilful players who just wanted to show off. Not good enough! Sometimes, Malcolm found hard-working players who just wanted to run. Not good enough!

Discovering 'a Manchester United player' was like a treasure hunt. There were lots of twists and wrong-turns along the way, but it was all totally worth it in the end.

Fortunately, with Malcolm watching, David played one of the best games of his life. He was everywhere. In attack, he used his full range of passes and crosses to drive Waltham Forest forward and set up goals. There was plenty of skill but no showing off. Every touch was calm, clever and accurate.

'An eleven-year-old kid who can play a perfect thirty-yard pass,' Malcolm noted in his head. 'Now that's special!'

In defence, David worked hard for his team, tracking back to stop the Redbridge left-back. Despite his small size, he battled bravely to win every ball.

As he came to the touchline to take a throw-in, Malcolm could see the total focus on his face.

The scout was blown away. 'That kid is a Manchester United player!' he decided, even before half-time.

At full time, Malcolm went over to introduce himself to David's mum. 'Hi there, I work for Manchester United,' he began.

That was enough to give Sandra goosebumps. She tried to listen carefully, but she was too excited to take everything in.

'Your son is exactly the kind of player that we're looking for,' Malcolm went on, 'and I'd like him to come to Manchester for a trial.'

David drifted slowly out of the dressing room as usual. As he got into the car, he looked over at his mum's beaming face.

'What's going on?' he asked.

'You picked a good day to play like that!' Sandra told him. She looked like she was about to burst.

'Why?'

His mum pointed out of the window. 'That man

over there is a Manchester United scout!'

David checked that it wasn't a cruel joke and then punched the air with joy. He had been waiting so long to hear those words, so long that he had started to think that it might never happen. But now his dream was finally coming true! He wanted to share his news with the whole world, but with one person in particular.

'When we get home, can I call Dad?' he asked.

Malcolm drove David up to Manchester himself. At first, they didn't say much but three hours was a long time to sit in silence, and so they began to make small talk.

'Have you been to Old Trafford before?' Malcolm asked.

David nodded. 'I played on the pitch last year, actually.'

The scout seemed surprised. 'What competition was that?'

'The Bobby Charlton Soccer School skills competition. We went on before the United vs Spurs game and there must have been about forty thousand people watching us.'

'Well, this trial should be a walk in the park, then!' Malcolm laughed.

Soon enough, David would be involved in another United vs Spurs battle.

David had the time of his life, playing football, football and more football. Luckily, his energy was endless. The trip made him even more certain about moving to Manchester United.

'Dad, it's unbelievable here!' he raved on the phone. When he got home, he couldn't stop talking about his Old Trafford adventure.

After that first trial, David was called back for another one, and then another one. He had clearly impressed the coaches, but had he done enough to join their youth team permanently? That was the big question that gave David sleepless nights.

A few weeks later, the home phone rang. Ted answered it and when he returned, he looked like he'd seen a ghost.

'Who was it, Dad?' David asked.

'That was Alex Ferguson himself,' Ted replied,

hardly able to believe his own words. 'He said that you're exactly the kind of player that Manchester United are looking for.'

David jumped up off the sofa and ran around the room in circles like he was three years old again. Back then, he had been excited about his first Manchester United shirt. Now, he was excited about his first Manchester United contract. It was an incredible feeling to know that his favourite club in the world wanted him.

'So, what happens now?' he asked his dad. 'When do I sign?'

Ted shrugged. 'I'm not sure, son.'

Thankfully, Manchester United didn't lose interest in David. The club invited him and his parents to a team dinner in London. David sat near Ferguson for the whole meal, waiting for the right moment to give him his gift. Finally, he plucked up the courage.

'Wow, thanks, David,' the manager said, taking the pen out of its box. 'What a lovely gift! I'm going to use this pen to sign you for Manchester United.'

David's smile lasted days. He just wished that he

had recorded Ferguson's amazing words. Luckily, he had remembered them off by heart to tell his friends.

As his thirteenth birthday drew near, David had a decision to make. He was enjoying himself at Tottenham and they offered him a brilliant six-year deal. By the age of eighteen, he would be a professional footballer.

'So, are you ready to sign?' the Tottenham manager Terry Venables asked him.

David paused. He knew that it would make his grandad happy, but he needed to hear Manchester United's offer first. 'I'd like to think about it, please.'

After a quick handshake, Ferguson got straight down to business. 'We want to offer you a six-year deal,' he announced.

David looked over at his dad, who looked like he was about to collapse with shock and pride.

'I want to sign,' David said quickly. He didn't need time to think it over. This was the only club for him.

Ferguson smiled and took out the pen that David had given him as a gift. 'Welcome to Manchester United!'

CHAPTER 6

THE CLASS OF '92

Signing for Manchester United was a big step for David, but it was still only the first step. David was only thirteen and he still had a long journey ahead of him if he wanted to achieve his dream of playing for the first team.

'Don't start thinking you've made it yet,' his dad liked to remind him.

For the next two years, David stayed at home in London, playing football for Ridgeway Rovers as normal. Malcolm was there to keep an eye on him and report back to Old Trafford.

'I hope you told Fergie about that free kick I scored!' David told him with a cheeky grin.

It was only during the school holidays that he spent time in Manchester. The club invited him to come up for training camps.

'How long can I stay?' David asked eagerly. 'A month? Six weeks?'

Malcolm laughed. 'Sorry, it's just a week this time!'

Going away for the summer was fun, but going away for good? That was a lot tougher, but when he turned fifteen, it was time for David to leave home.

'Remember, you can call us at any time,' Sandra told him, trying not to cry in front of him. 'Day or night!'

'Enjoy yourself, son!' Ted said, giving him a hearty hug.

At times, David did miss his family, but they came up to watch him play every weekend. And normally, he was too busy enjoying himself to think of home. When he wasn't playing football, he was going to the cinema and hanging out with his new mates.

All of the boys who weren't from Manchester lived together in boarding houses. They had a landlady who looked after them, but most of the time, they were free to explore. There was John O'Kane from Nottingham, Robbie Savage from Wales, and Keith Gillespie all the way from Ireland.

'If we stick together, maybe the other lads won't make fun of our accents!' they decided.

Those other lads included a group who had played together for years at a local team called Boundary Park. The Neville brothers, Gary and Phil, played in defence, Nicky Butt played in midfield and Paul Scholes was an attacker. They were a tight-knit bunch but, thanks to football, David was soon allowed to join their gang.

'Here comes the London lad again!' they liked to joke, putting on awful Cockney voices.

'Thanks, now I feel right at home!' David joked back.

As soon as training started, however, the laughter stopped. The Manchester United youth coach, Eric Harrison, was like Stuart, David's manager at Ridgeway Rovers. He expected 100 per cent effort and commitment at all times.

'There are millions of kids out there who would love to be in your position,' Eric told his young stars. 'Don't waste this chance!'

If anyone dared to mess around, they were in big trouble. Even if he wasn't there with them on the field, Eric was usually watching them through the window of his office. If he saw something he didn't like, he would bang furiously on the glass.

That sound was something the players all dreaded. 'Uh-oh!' they'd say, looking down at their feet guiltily.

Eric knew how to get the best out of each and every one of them. He was always looking for ways to improve his young players and help them to achieve their full potential. Eric wasn't worried about David's work rate. He knew that he would run up and down the wing all day long in order to win a football match.

Instead, Eric worked on his decision making. Sometimes, the simple pass was the best pass, rather than trying to strike it sixty yards. David's midfield hero was England's classy playmaker, Glenn Hoddle, but football couldn't always be that beautiful.

'Stop going for those Hollywood balls every time!' Eric shouted angrily on the touchline.

When the practice finished, he went over to offer David more advice. 'Get the basics right first. Watch Bryan Robson – watch what he does.'

With Eric's guidance and Robson's example, David got better and better. He still loved playing long passes but he had to pick the right moments to use that remarkable right foot of his.

Gary Neville was just as determined and they often stayed behind to do extra practice together. After training in the morning and training in the afternoon, they would then train with the schoolboys in the evening.

'You lads will go far with an attitude like that!' Eric told them.

That was exactly what they were hoping. Another Manchester United youngster, Ryan Giggs, was already on his way to becoming a first-team star. That gave David and Gary the confidence to keep chasing their dream.

David needed that self-belief because he had a battle on his hands. Keith played on the right wing too and in the big FA Youth Cup matches, he was Eric's first choice. How could David force his way into the starting line-up? By doing what he always did – working hard and creating goals.

Eventually, Eric had no option but to move Keith up front and bring David into the team. After playing well against Tottenham in the semi-final, he stayed there for the final against Crystal Palace.

'Yes!' David shouted when he saw his name there on the teamsheet, alongside Gary, John, Robbie and Nicky. 'Come on, let's win this, lads!'

On a soaking wet Selhurst Park pitch, Nicky gave Manchester United the lead. Then, after thirty minutes, the ball came towards David on the edge of the penalty area. There was no time to think or take a touch. He smashed a vicious left-foot volley past the keeper.

Gooooooooooooooooooooaaaaaaaaaaaaaaaaalllllllllllll llllllllllllll!!!!!!!!!!!!!!!!!!!!

It took a moment to sink in but once it did, it

was the greatest moment of David's life. Adrenaline flooded his body and he felt like he could run forever. He raced towards the corner, with his teammates chasing behind.

'Becks, I didn't even know you had a left foot!' Gary teased as they celebrated.

For the second leg at Old Trafford, they had 30,000 fans cheering them on. Word was spreading about the club's amazing 'Class of '92'.

'Don't get ahead of yourselves, they're just here to see me!' Giggsy joked. He was back to captain the team to victory.

Once it started, David didn't want the match to ever end. What a night! The atmosphere was amazing. He was playing football with his friends for his favourite club in the world in front of a roaring crowd. Could life get any better than that?

Yes, with a trophy! As Giggsy lifted the FA Youth Cup high into the sky, David stood right behind him. When it was David's turn, he raised it towards his proud parents. He had so much to thank them for.

'This is the best youth team I've ever worked with,' Eric told the media.

Alex Ferguson was there at Old Trafford too to congratulate the Class of '92. In the dressing room, he looked around at the future first-team stars – Giggsy, Gary, Nicky and David. The right winger wasn't the most highly-rated member of the team, but Ferguson could see the pure ambition in his eyes.

'That boy is going to be a top, top player,' the Manchester United manager thought to himself.

CHAPTER 7

TESTING TIMES

After his key role in Manchester United's FA Youth Cup victory, David looked destined for the big time. How long would it be before he joined the first team?

David made his senior team debut a few months later in the League Cup against Brighton and Hove Albion. With twenty minutes to go, he came on to replace Andrei Kanchelskis on the right wing.

'Run your socks off and get some crosses into the box,' Ferguson instructed him.

David did exactly that. By the final whistle, he was exhausted, but his whole body was buzzing. He could really call himself a Manchester United player now.

'How was it?' his dad asked.

David didn't have the words to describe the feeling. 'Unbelievable!' he went for in the end, but it didn't do it justice.

When David signed his first professional contract in January 1993, he could see his Manchester United journey in front of him. From the youth team, he would go to the reserves, then to the first team squad, and finally to the starting line-up.

In his head, it was going to be a rapid rise, but it didn't turn out that way. He would have to wait two whole years to make his full debut.

In the meantime, he played lots of games for the reserves and he played in a second FA Youth Cup Final. He lined up in midfield with Nicky. Gary was the captain at the back, and Paul Scholes was up front.

'Let's win this, lads!' Gary shouted confidently.

It looked like another strong Manchester United team, but they were no match for Leeds. Wearing the Number 8 shirt, David did his best to create chances for his team, but it was difficult on a boggy, bobbling pitch. Every time he crossed the ball into the box, the big Leeds defenders headed it away.

'Simple passes!' Eric screamed on the touchline.

At the final whistle, David trudged off through the mud. It was a year on from their success against Crystal Palace, and it didn't feel like he was getting any closer to the first team. These were testing times for a young footballer.

'Be patient,' his dad told him. 'You've only just turned eighteen!'

'I know, but Giggsy is already playing week in, week out for the first team. When am I going to get my chance?'

'Trust me, you'll get your chance soon, son.'

The 1993–94 season came and went but as the next season arrived, things were looking up for David. Ferguson gave him his first start in the League Cup against Port Vale. There were four members of the Class of '92 on the teamsheet – David, Nicky, Gary and Scholesy. It was their big chance to shine and impress their manager.

'We need to do a better job than we did against

Leeds,' Gary said on the way to the game.

'That won't be hard, especially for you!' Nicky joked back.

On the night, Scholesy was United's hero with two brilliant goals. David was really pleased for his friend, but he couldn't help feeling a little bit jealous too. With Fergie watching on, he had failed to be his team's stand-out star. The others were leaving him behind.

Would David get another chance? He played in the next round against Newcastle, but they lost 2–0.

And another? In December, he was in the squad for the Champions League game against Galatasaray. There were rumours in the newspapers that the manager was going to give his youngsters a chance, but David didn't want to get his hopes up. It was best to assume that he was on the bench.

That all changed on match day, however, when Ferguson read out the teamsheet:

'…Number Seven: Cantona, Eight: Butt, Nine:. McClair, Ten: Beckham, Eleven: Davies…'

'We're starting!' Nicky whispered happily.

David couldn't believe it. His parents were going to be in the crowd but there was no time to tell them the exciting news. So they were in for a shock when they saw their son walking out at Old Trafford with Steve Bruce, Denis Irwin, Brian McClair and Eric Cantona.

Suddenly, David was very nervous about making his European debut. What if he missed an important tackle, or gave the ball away for Galatasaray to score?

'Good luck, lad,' Roy Keane said, giving him a slap on the back. 'Show the fans what you're made of!'

Brian chased after a long goal kick, but a defender slid in for the tackle. As the ball bounced out to the edge of the penalty area, David sprinted towards it as fast as he could. He won the race and shot past the diving goalkeeper.

Goooooooooooooooooooooaaaaaaaaaaaaaaaaaallllllllllllll llllllllllllllll!!!!!!!!!!!!!!!!!!!

The ball seemed to roll into back of the net in slow motion. Surely, it was too good to be true? But no, it was true – David had scored in his first ever

Champions League game. His smile kept growing bigger and bigger. Before he knew what he was doing, he was jumping into Eric's arms. Luckily, his French teammate didn't seem to mind.

David came back down to earth with a bang. A few weeks after scoring at Old Trafford, he was off to play for Preston North End in the Third Division.

'You're just going there on loan for a month,' Ferguson reassured him. 'Hopefully, it will toughen you up a bit. Think of it as a valuable experience and a chance to get some more games under your belt. You'll be back here in no time!'

David couldn't help worrying about his United future, but he had to trust his manager and focus on impressing at Preston. He didn't get off to a good start, however.

'This is David Beckham, he's on loan from Manchester United,' the manager, Gary Peters, told his team. 'He'll be taking all our free kicks and corners from now on.'

The senior players weren't happy at all. When David came on for his debut against Doncaster, Paul

Raynor had to come off. He sat down moodily on the bench. 'Who does that kid think he is?' he muttered to himself.

A few minutes later, David swung a high corner all the way into the net.

Goooooooooooooooooooooaaaaaaaaaaaaaaaaalllllllllllll llllllllllllllll!!!!!!!!!!!!!!!!!!!!

In his second game, David curled one of his trademark free kicks up over the wall and into the top corner.

Goooooooooooooooooooooaaaaaaaaaaaaaaaaalllllllllllll llllllllllllllll!!!!!!!!!!!!!!!!!!!!

After that, Raynor kept quiet. Everyone at Preston could see that David was the real deal. It wasn't just his good looks and natural talent; it was also all the hard work that he did on the training ground. Every day, he stayed behind to do extra practice – free kicks, corners, passes.

'Teacher's pet,' the players called him.

It was all friendly banter, though. On the way to one game, David was sat on his own, reading an article about himself in *Match* magazine, when

Raymond Sharp looked over and snatched it out of his hands.

'Hey, give it back!'

'"Scoring in Europe was a moment that I will never forget",' Sharp read out loud for everyone to enjoy. He even tried to imitate David's London accent. '"When the ball crossed the line, I ran into Eric's arms. It was wonderful."'

David's face was bright red as laughter rang out all over the team bus. Sharp handed the magazine back to him with a wink. 'Just remember us when you're winning the Premier League!'

After two goals in five games, it was time for David to return to Manchester United. 'Good luck, guys!' he called out to the Preston players as he waved goodbye.

'Thanks, we're going to need it without you!' the players replied.

Back at Old Trafford, David finally made his Premier League debut in April 1995 against Leeds United. Even a dull 0–0 draw couldn't dampen his spirits.

'I can't believe I played the full ninety minutes!' he told his parents proudly.

'Fergie must be impressed!' his mum replied, sounding just as proud.

David's confidence grew with more game time against Leicester City, Chelsea and Coventry City. He was almost a regular now.

Manchester United finished the 1994–95 season without a single trophy. Blackburn won the Premier League and Everton won the FA Cup. There was lots of gloom around Old Trafford that summer, but David was feeling positive. His time had arrived.

CHAPTER 8

FERGIE'S FLEDGLINGS

Just as the 1995–96 Premier League season started, Andrei Kanchelskis left Manchester United to join Everton. The Russian winger was the third senior player to leave that summer, after Paul Ince and Mark Hughes. What was going on at Old Trafford, and why wasn't Ferguson buying new players to replace them?

The answer was that the Manchester United manager believed in his new young stars, the Class of '92. He believed that there was no need to replace Ince and Kanchelskis when he already had Giggsy, Scholesy, Nicky and David. The club's future looked very bright indeed.

With Kanchelskis gone, David was now only battling with Lee Sharpe for the right-wing spot.

'This is going to be my season,' David told Gary Neville confidently. 'I know it!'

In the first match against Aston Villa, it was Lee who started alongside Gary, Phil, Nicky and Scholesy. David was disappointed to be the one on the bench, but at half-time, United were losing 3–0.

'Get ready, kid,' Ferguson told him. 'You're coming on.'

David wanted to smile but he didn't. It wasn't a time for smiling; it was a time for focusing. He had forty-five minutes to show that he was good enough to start the next match. He ran and ran, covering every blade of grass on the pitch.

David took the corners, he took the free kicks, and he curled other crosses into the box too. But with ten minutes to go, it was still 3–0 to Aston Villa. When Roy Keane passed to him, David chested the ball down and decided to go for goal. His shot sailed high and wide.

'Hahahaha!' the Villa fans laughed.

But David didn't let that knock his confidence. The next time the ball came to him, he controlled it beautifully, took a touch to steady himself, and then unleashed a powerful, swerving strike.

Mark Bosnich was having a good game in the Villa goal, but he had no chance of saving this one. He could only turn his head to watch it hit the top corner.

Goooooooooooooooooooooaaaaaaaaaaaaaaaaaalllllllllllll lllllllllllllll!!!!!!!!!!!!!!!!!!!!!!

David was delighted with his first Premier League goal but he didn't really celebrate because United were still losing 3–1. The fans, however, stood and clapped their new scorer. There were just glad to have one positive to take from their team's nightmare start.

'Ferguson needs to buy players,' former Liverpool player Alan Hansen told the British public on *Match of the Day*. 'You can't win anything with kids.'

'We'll see about that!' was the team's response to Hansen's prediction.

After his goal against Aston Villa, David started

the next match and the next and the next. With Eric
Cantona and Giggsy missing, the manager played
David, Lee and Scholesy in the same attack. 'Fergie's
Fledglings' worked brilliantly together.

Against West Ham, Lee played a long pass to
Scholesy, who passed to David, who passed to Nicky.
Nicky passed to Lee, who flicked it to Keano, who
scored. 2–1! As Keano threw himself down on the
grass, all of his teammates piled on top of him.

Against Premier League Champions Blackburn,
Lee scored the first goal but could United grab the
winner too? With the ball bouncing around in the
box, it was going to take a moment of calm and
class. Up stepped David to curl a first-time shot past
the keeper.

*Goooooooooooooooooooooaaaaaaaaaaaaaaaaaallllllllllllll
lllllllllllllll!!!!!!!!!!!!!!!!!!!!!*

What an important strike! David threw his arms
up in the air and ran towards the United fans by the
corner flag. He was having the best time ever.

'You're not just a pretty face!' Keano joked,
slapping him playfully on the cheek.

Ferguson ran along the touchline, punching the air. His youngsters were doing him proud.

Things got even better when Giggsy returned. With a Welsh wing wizard on the left and an English wing wizard on the right, United were unstoppable. Giggsy dribbled past defenders for fun and David delivered dangerous cross after cross. Together, they caused so many problems for Premier League defences.

United jumped ahead of Newcastle at the top of the table. It soon became a thrilling two-horse title race – 'Fergie's Fledglings' versus Kevin Keegan's Entertainers. Who would lift the trophy in May? David was as determined as ever. He had achieved his dream of becoming a United player but now, he was on to the next dream – winning trophies.

At Old Trafford, Glenn Hoddle's Chelsea took the lead. It was a match that United couldn't afford to lose because Newcastle were already five points clear. The ball came to David on the edge of the penalty area. He didn't have much time or space to shoot but, in a flash, he lifted the ball over the mass of blue shirts and into the top corner.

*Goooooooooooooooooooooaaaaaaaaaaaaaaaaaalllllllllllll
lllllllllllllll!!!!!!!!!!!!!!!!!!!!*

David jumped for joy. At the age of twenty, he was
quickly becoming a key part of the United team.

In the FA Cup semi-final, he scored another
goal against Chelsea and this time, it was the
matchwinner. David chased after Craig Burley's
sloppy back-pass and steered the ball past the keeper.
2–1! The United fans behind the goal bounced up
and down with delight.

'You hero, Becks!' Nicky screamed. 'We're off to
Wembley!'

Before the FA Cup Final, United had a league title
to win. By April, they were top of the table again
and there weren't budging for anyone. David scored
his seventh and eighth goals of the season in a 5–0
thrashing of Nottingham Forest. After that first goal
against Aston Villa, he had never looked back.

'Great, now we just need a draw at
Middlesbrough,' Gary explained. With one point,
United would be crowned champions.

Giggsy shook his head. The Class of '92 didn't

believe in draws. He still remembered that awful draw at West Ham that handed the 1994–95 title to Blackburn. They had to get it right this time. 'No way, we're going for the win as usual!'

Giggsy inspired United to a 3–0 victory. A plane flew over the Riverside Stadium, celebrating the big news: 'MANCHESTER UNITED: CARLING CHAMPIONS'. At the final whistle, 'Fergie's Fledglings' jumped up and down together – they had achieved the impossible!

David had his first senior trophy, the first of many he hoped. What an amazing breakthrough season 1995–96 had been – 39 matches and 8 goals. It was beyond his wildest dreams. He ran over to thank his manager.

'I feel like a very proud father!' Fergie said as his youngsters hugged him. 'I believed in you guys – and boy, did you repay my faith!'

United weren't done yet – the kids had something else to win. They completed The Double at Wembley by beating Liverpool 1–0. As he lifted the FA Cup high above his head, David felt on top of the world.

CHAPTER 9

THE WIMBLEDON WONDERSTRIKE

As the 1996–97 season kicked off, there were so many questions about the Manchester United team. Was their Premier League title win from the previous season a fluke, a one-off? Could they really keep winning things with kids? And just how good were 'Fergie's Fledglings' anyway?

'Very, very good' was the answer, and they were only just getting started. David was pleased with his progress, but one season wasn't enough. He was determined to go on and establish himself as a superstar. He was already thinking about his next dream – playing for England.

After a summer holiday in Italy, he couldn't wait
to get back to football.

'The hard work begins today,' Ferguson told
his players before the away trip to tough-tackling
Wimbledon. 'We're the champions now and that
means that everyone is going to want to beat us.
Teams are going to try to foul you, cheat you, scare
you – anything to win. But don't let them!'

In the tunnel, the Wimbledon captain Vinnie Jones
grinned his most fiendish grin. 'Welcome kids, I hope
you're ready for this!'

Jones and his 'Crazy Gang' wanted to teach
United's skilful youngsters a lesson or two, but
David wasn't scared. He was twenty-one years old
and fearless. He had been taking on bigger boys
for years.

He took his place on the right wing, proudly
wearing the United Number 10 shirt. It was a big
upgrade from Number 24. He had worked hard to
earn it and now it was time to prove that he should
keep it. If he didn't, the club's new Czech signing,
Karel Poborský, was waiting on the bench.

David's shirt number wasn't the only thing that was new. Adidas had sent him a pair of their latest Predator boots. They looked awesome and they felt awesome, even if they did have the wrong footballer's name written on the red tongues.

'Alright, Charlie!' Nicky joked.

'I can't believe I've been getting your name wrong for all these years,' Scholesy teased. 'Sorry about that, Charlie!'

David laughed along, knowing that a goal would soon shut his friends up.

'Let's do this!' captain Eric roared. He expected 110 per cent effort from his teammates.

With the sun shining brightly, David got stuck in straight away. He raced back to win the ball off Oyvind Leonhardsen and then passed to Keano. Seconds later, it was in the back of the net. 1–0 to United!

As Eric stood and raised his arms up in the air, David, Paul, Nicky and Phil all rushed over to celebrate with their leader. The team was one big, happy family.

With seconds to go, United were cruising to a 2–0 victory. Ronny Johnsen tackled Efan Ekoku and passed to Brian McClair, who poked the ball forward to David just inside his own half. As he looked up for someone to pass to, he spotted that the Wimbledon goalkeeper, Neil Sullivan, was off his line.

'Why not?' David thought to himself.

He had scored lots of long-range goals before and it was a brilliant chance to test his new Predator boots. Surely, Ferguson wouldn't mind him having a go in the last minute of the match?

'Not another Hollywood ball!' David could imagine his old Manchester youth coach shouting.

But he knew that he could do it. He had done it lots of times in training, so why not in a real match? Just before he reached the halfway line, he swung his left arm backwards, and his remarkable right foot forwards. Bang! It looked more like a pass, but that was just David's special, shooting technique. He knew exactly what he was doing.

The stadium fell silent. All eyes watched the ball

as it flew towards the Wimbledon goal. Surely, it couldn't? Could it? It seemed to hang in the air for hours.

At first, Sullivan jogged backwards just in case. But as the ball began to drop, he turned and panicked. He jumped up to try to save it, but he was too late. It landed in the back of the net.

Gooooooooooooooooooooaaaaaaaaaaaaaaaaallllllllllll lllllllllllllll!!!!!!!!!!!!!!!!!!!!!

The Manchester United fans behind the goal were up on their feet, going wild. They couldn't believe what they had just seen. Their midfielder maestro had just scored from the halfway line!

David stood and raised his arms up in the air like Eric. He tried to look cool, but he couldn't stop the smile from spreading across his face. It was the proudest moment of his career so far. What a way to start the new season!

'Take a bow, David Beckham!' commentator Martin Tyler cheered on TV.

'Charlie, you're a genius!' Scholesy screamed.

Eric was a man of few words but even he went

over to congratulate his teammate. 'What a goal,' he said, with a nod of respect.

David beamed with joy. It meant so much to hear those words from his captain, and his manager's words were even better.

'We've just seen the goal of the season already,' Ferguson told the media. 'I have never seen anyone do that before. Pelé is the only one who came close.'

The next day, the newspapers had a big question for their readers – 'Was That the Greatest Goal Ever?'

David was already a famous face in England, but suddenly, people knew about him all over the world. With that Wimbledon wonderstrike, David took a giant leap towards his dream of becoming a footballing superstar. It was a goal that changed his life forever.

CHAPTER 10

EXCITING NEW ERA FOR ENGLAND

What next for Manchester United's young star? His senior international debut!

After losing to Germany in the semi-finals of Euro 96, England needed some fresh new talent. David fitted the bill perfectly, especially after his recent Wimbledon Wonderstrike. He was a Premier League Champion and a classy midfield playmaker.

'Get Becks in the squad!' the country cried out. 'The World Cup is only two years away!'

The new national team manager was Glenn Hoddle, David's childhood hero. What changes would he make for his first match in charge against Moldova? England were looking to start off their

World Cup qualification campaign with a bang.

David was sat at home, relaxing with his mum, when he checked the football news on TV. Hoddle had just named his squad and his eyes scanned over the names. Gary was in, alongside Stuart Pearce, Gareth Southgate, Paul Ince, David Beckha–

'Mum, look!' David screamed, jumping off the sofa. 'I'm in the England squad!'

After a quick hug, he phoned his dad at work to give him the great news. At first, Ted was speechless.

'Son, that's fantastic!' he managed to say eventually.

Alex Ferguson was delighted too. 'Congratulations! Just play like you've been playing for United, and you'll be fine.'

As he arrived at the national team camp, however, David felt like a little kid again. He was twenty-one years old now but he had grown up watching many of his new international teammates on TV – David Seaman, Paul Gascoigne, Alan Shearer. He felt star-struck.

'Don't just stand there, Becks,' Gary shouted over. 'Get warmed up!'

Once he had the ball at his feet, David remembered Fergie's message – 'Just play like you've been playing for United.'

No problem! With his remarkable right foot, David made sure that every pass and every cross was absolutely perfect. He was so focused on football that he soon forgot who he was playing with.

Hoddle was impressed and named him in the starting line-up. It was an exciting new era for England, and for David.

David thought back to the age of twelve, when a youth coach told him that he would never play for his country.

'Sorry lad, you're too small and weak.'

He thought back to missing out on the England squad for the Under-18 Euros back in 1993.

'Sorry lad, you didn't make the cut this time.'

Those disappointments had only spurred him on to keep going, to keep proving people wrong.

All of that hard work had been worth it. David had progressed from the England Under-18s to the Under-21s, and now he was about to make his senior debut.

'This is amazing!' he told Gary, who was also in the team. 'We're going to rule the right wing!'

In David's childhood dreams, he would have made his debut at Wembley, the Home of Football, in front of 80,000 cheering fans. In reality, there were fewer than 10,000 fans in Moldova's national stadium, but he wore the Three Lions on his shirt and that was all that mattered. After singing the national anthem loud and proud, it was time for David to kick off his England career.

In the end, it was a solid but unspectacular debut. Although he didn't score any wonderstrikes, he looked confident on the ball and never stopped running. With a 3–0 win, David and the exciting new England era were both up and running.

'Well played,' Hoddle said to him at the final whistle. 'How did that feel?'

'Incredible!' David replied, trying to catch his breath.

Now, he just needed to make sure that he kept his place. In the next match against Poland, he dribbled forward, over the halfway line.

'Shoot!' the fans shouted.

Not this time. Instead, he looked up and chipped a long diagonal cross towards Alan Shearer. It was inch-perfect. Alan had the easy job of heading it past the goalkeeper.

'Great ball!' he cheered, giving David a high-five.

It was a real relief to get his first England assist but what about that first England goal? David scored lots of free kicks for his club, so why not for his country?

'You'll get one soon,' Hoddle reassured him in training. 'We've got lots of other goalscorers, though, so don't worry about that. What I want from you is lots of crossing and passing, and you're doing that brilliantly!'

Slowly but surely, Fergie's Fledglings were taking over the England team. By the time Moldova came to Wembley, there were five of them in the team – Gary and Phil in defence, and David, Scholesy and Nicky in midfield. To celebrate, David whipped in a dangerous ball and Scholesy scored with a diving header.

'World Cup, here we come!' David cheered as he

jumped on his Manchester United teammate.

With a hard-fought 0–0 draw in Italy, the Three Lions had qualified for the 1998 World Cup in France. At the final whistle, the players all ran over to celebrate with the supporters.

England! England! England!

What a feeling – David was a national hero now. If he kept playing like he'd been playing for United, he would soon be off to the World Cup in France.

CHAPTER 11

POSH AND BECKS

David was making a name for himself at Manchester United, both on and off the pitch.

On the pitch, David wasn't just scoring goals for his club; he was scoring *brilliant* goals.

Against Derby, he dribbled forward and fired a great shot past the goalkeeper.

Goooooooooooooooooooaaaaaaaaaaaaaaaalllllllllllll llllllllllllll!!!!!!!!!!!!!!!!!!!!

Against Southampton, he curled a fierce free kick up over the wall and into the top corner.

Goooooooooooooooooooaaaaaaaaaaaaaaaalllllllllllll llllllllllllll!!!!!!!!!!!!!!!!!!!!

And David wasn't just scoring brilliant goals for his

club; he was scoring brilliant and *important* goals. He scored the winners against Liverpool and Tottenham and the equaliser against Chelsea. He was becoming a big game player.

Off the pitch, meanwhile, David was now one half of England's hottest celebrity couple.

The music group, the Spice Girls, had taken the country by storm. There were five members, all with different personalities: Sporty Spice, Scary Spice, Ginger Spice, Baby Spice – and then Posh Spice, Victoria Adams.

Everyone had their favourite Spice Girl, especially David. 'Posh is perfect,' he told Gary as they watched music videos together on TV. 'She's so beautiful and stylish. She's the one for me!'

But how would he get to meet the girl of his dreams? Luckily, after a Manchester United game against Chelsea, David found out that two of the Spice Girls were up in the Players' Lounge.

'Which ones?' he asked frantically.

No-one knew the answer, so he rushed to find out for himself. It turned out to be Posh and Sporty. As he started speaking to them, he was so nervous that he could feel the sweat trickling down his forehead. Playing football in front of 70,000 fans at Old Trafford was nothing compared to this.

'Hello, I'm David,' he said.

'Hello, I'm Victoria,' she said.

And that was it. David froze – he didn't know what to say next. He was tongue-tied, and he couldn't take his eyes off her.

Victoria wasn't much of a football fan, but she was a big fan of David. A week later, she travelled from London to Manchester just to watch a match at Old Trafford. Afterwards, she was there in the Players' Lounge, waiting for him.

When he saw Victoria there, David's heart nearly leapt out of his chest. He stood talking to his parents for a while, trying to calm himself down. The last thing he wanted to do was make a fool of himself for a second time.

Eventually, however, David plucked up the courage to go over and speak to her. He was nervous at first but once he relaxed, they chatted for ages about fame, their families and growing up in Essex. They had lots in common and made each other laugh.

This time, before she left to go home, Victoria asked for David's phone number. He was crazy about her, but what if she lost the scrap of paper and never called? He didn't want to take that risk.

'No, I'll take yours,' David decided.

'Okay,' Victoria replied with a smile, writing it on the back of an old plane ticket. 'Let me know when you're next in London!'

When he got home, David wrote the number down in lots of different places, just to be safe. He called her as soon as he woke up the next day.

'Victoria? It's David.'

For the first few months, David and Victoria managed to keep their relationship a secret. That wasn't easy for two famous people, but it gave them time to really get to know each other. David's phone bill got bigger and bigger each week, as did the bouquets of flowers that he sent to Victoria.

'Who's your secret admirer?' her sister Louise asked.

'A guy in Manchester,' was all Victoria would say.

When they went on dates, they chose random places, far from the public eye. No matter where they met, though, David always made sure that his car looked sparkling clean. He was eager to impress Victoria and they spent hours talking over romantic, candlelit dinners.

'We haven't hung out for ages!' Gary complained at training one day.

'Sorry, I've been busy,' David replied.

'Busy with what? You're always in a good mood these days. Have you got a girlfriend?'

David stayed silent.

'You have, haven't you!' Gary teased. 'Who is she, then? Anyone I know?'

Should he just say, 'a girl from London'? No, he wanted to tell his best friend the truth. After another short silence, David revealed his secret. 'Victoria Adams.'

Gary looked confused.

'Posh Spice,' David explained.

Their relationship was soon front page news. Suddenly, the paparazzi followed them everywhere, even when they walked their dogs down the street.

'Posh and Becks' were the talk of the UK.

David had always liked to look stylish but now that he was a celebrity footballer, he had to look stylish all the time. Not only that, but he also had to keep changing his style all the time too. Otherwise, his fans would get bored and move on to a new heartthrob. David started slicking his hair back with gel and then dyed it blonde.

As soon as he arrived at training, his teammates mocked him mercilessly.

'Blimey, I thought this was a sports team, not a boyband!'

'Before you ask, no I'm not joining the Spice Boys!'

'These days, you spend longer in front of the mirror than you do on the football pitch!'

David smiled and laughed along. Just as long as he was playing well for Manchester United, he could do whatever he liked in his private life.

In May 1997, David won his second Premier League title and the PFA Young Player of the Year award. In January 1998, he asked Victoria to marry him. She said yes.

CHAPTER 12

A MOMENT OF MADNESS

With so much media attention on David at home, it was nice for him to escape for the summer. He was off to France, but it wasn't for a holiday – it was for the 1998 World Cup. He couldn't wait to play in his first major international tournament.

Growing up, David had been England's biggest fan. He'd cheered on Bryan Robson and Glenn Hoddle in 1982, Gary Lineker in 1986 and then Gazza in 1990. Eight years on, David was the one representing his country at the World Cup.

'It's going to be awesome!' he told Gary and Scholesy.

Gary had played at Euro 96 but Scholesy had even

fewer England caps than David. The three of them were representing Manchester United's Class of '92. Nicky and Phil hadn't been picked, while Giggsy had chosen to play for Wales instead.

'He'll never admit it, but he must really regret that decision!' Scholesy joked.

England went into the World Cup with high hopes. There was lots of talent and experience in the team's core – David Seaman in goal, Tony Adams in defence, Paul Ince in midfield and Alan Shearer in attack.

But Hoddle had also picked lots of exciting young players. Fergie's Fledglings were joined by Tottenham's Sol Campbell, West Ham's Rio Ferdinand and, most exciting of all, Liverpool's eighteen-year-old striker Michael Owen.

'I'm glad he's on our team this time,' Gary admitted. 'He's absolutely rapid!'

David and Gary were both on the bench for the first game against Tunisia. Darren Anderton played at right wing-back, putting them both out of a position. They watched and waited, melting in the Marseille heat. But their chance never came because Alan and Scholesy scored to give England the victory.

'What a strike, mate!' David congratulated his friend.

'Yeah, but what about that miss in the first-half, Scholesy?' Gary teased.

Hoddle brought Gary into the team against Romania, but he still left David on the bench. This wasn't how he'd imagined his first World Cup, especially as he had played every single qualifying game. After thirty minutes, however, Paul Ince injured his ankle. He had to go off, but who would come on to replace him? David!

David tucked in his baggy Number 7 shirt and ran on to the field. He had achieved yet another childhood dream – playing for England at the World Cup. But before he could really get into the game, Romania took the lead.

'Come on!' Seaman cried out in frustration.

David did his best to set up the equaliser. He kept putting balls into the box for Alan and Teddy Sheringham to attack. The crosses were excellent, of course, but the goal didn't arrive. With twenty minutes to go, Michael came on for Teddy. Suddenly, England had some pace to play with.

David dribbled forward and played a great pass over the top to Alan. Alan smashed the ball across goal, but Scholesy couldn't quite control it. Luckily, Michael was right behind and ready to score. 1–1!

David raced over to hug England's goalscoring hero. 'What a super sub!' he cheered.

Michael grinned. 'Yeah and so are you. They've got to start us next time!'

Before that, however, Romania scored again to win the game. That meant England would have to beat Colombia in their final group game or be knocked out of the tournament.

'We can't let that happen!' captain Alan demanded.

Hoddle finally made the attacking changes that the English people were calling for. In came David and Michael to play with Alan, Scholesy and Darren. 'Go score some goals!' their manager shouted.

After twenty minutes, Darren slammed a rocket of

a shot into the roof of the net. 1–0! He ran over to David to celebrate.

'See Becks, of course we can play in the same team!'

Ten minutes later, England won a free kick in a good shooting position. David still hadn't scored for England, but his teammates believed in him. 'You've got this!' Darren told him.

'Yes, I've got this!' David told himself. He took a deep breath and imagined that he was back at Old Trafford, scoring another Premier League free kick. If he could do it there, he could do it anywhere.

As David ran forward, he swung his left arm backwards and his remarkable right foot forwards. Bang! The ball curled up over the wall and then dipped down into the bottom corner.

Goooooooooooooooooooooaaaaaaaaaaaaaaaaaallllllllllll llllllllllllllll!!!!!!!!!!!!!!!!!!

What a way for David to score his first England goal! He had been waiting a long time for this moment. How should he celebrate? He raced over to the fans behind the goal and stood in front of them, pumping his fists. Finally, his teammates caught up with him and Gary jumped up onto his back.

'Mate, that was unstoppable!' he cheered.

This was how David had imagined his first World Cup, full of goals and glory.

Next up in the second round, England faced their old rivals, Argentina. There was no question that David would start – he was the new national hero.

It turned out to be one of the most thrilling matches of the tournament. After ten minutes, it was already 1–1. David fed a great pass through for Michael to chase. The speedy striker was off, dribbling forward, past defender after defender. In the box, he finished off his wondergoal in style. 2–1 to England!

'You beauty!' David screamed.

It was all going so well for England. Too well. Just before half time, Argentina made it 2–2. Then just after half time, David went to chest the ball down, but Diego Simeone barged right into his back.

'Arghhhhh!' David cried out.

He was furious about the foul. As he lay on the floor, he kicked out at the Argentina midfielder's

legs. It was a moment of madness, right in front of
the referee. Simeone collapsed to the floor and David
was off. Red card!

What a mistake. He could see the disappointment
on his teammates' faces – Alan, Scholesy, Gary. But
he hadn't just let them down – he had let his whole
country down.

He didn't argue. He just turned and traipsed off
the pitch. It was the longest walk of his life. He could
feel so many eyes watching him, despising him for
what he had just done. He deserved it.

'What was I thinking? I did exactly what Simeone
hoped I would do. I'm so stupid!'

England's ten men held on, all the way to
penalties but in the shoot-out, Incey and David Batty
both missed. They were out of the World Cup.

David sat there in the dressing room, crying on
his own, waiting for his teammates to return. What
would they say? At first, there was total silence. Gary
and Scholesy came over and patted him on the back
but no-one said a word. Finally, Tony put an arm
around him and spoke.

'Look son, everyone makes mistakes,' he said. 'You're going to come back bigger and better, I promise.'

Those kind words meant a lot to him, but David was distraught. In the space of four days, he had gone from national hero to national villain.

'Ten Heroic Lions, One Stupid Boy,' one newspaper headline read.

As seemingly the most hated man in England, David was dreading his return from France. He would have to face horrible abuse, both through his letter box and in stadiums across the country. How was he going to deal with all that anger? He couldn't do it on his own. At that difficult time in his life, he needed support.

As soon as he finished speaking to his parents and Victoria, his phone rang again. It was his manager and mentor.

'Son, get back to Manchester,' Ferguson told him calmly. 'We'll look after you. You'll be fine.'

CHAPTER 13

THE TREBLE

Fergie was right – David would be fine. He just needed to focus on his football – winning more trophies with Manchester United, and then making things right with England.

'You're made of strong stuff,' his dad reminded him. 'Come back even stronger!'

David did just that. In the last minute of the first match of the 1998–99 season, Manchester United were losing 2–1. They won a free kick within shooting range.

'Is this going to be David Beckham's big moment?' the TV commentator asked.

Yes! The ball swerved and dipped into the bottom corner.

*Goooooooooooooooooooaaaaaaaaaaaaaaaalllllllllllll
lllllllllllll!!!!!!!!!!!!!!!!!!*

The Leicester fans carried on booing him, but David was back to being a Manchester United hero.

'Love him or hate him, you can't keep a great player down!' the TV commentator yelled over the Old Trafford noise.

David felt a wave of relief rush through his body. After his moment of madness at the World Cup, he had thought about leaving his childhood club and moving to Spain or Italy.

'Stay!' Keano had told him. 'We need you!'

David could never say no to his scary captain. He wasn't going anywhere, not yet. He couldn't just run away from trouble. There was more that he wanted to win at Manchester United. First of all, they needed to take the Premier League title back from Arsenal. After that, who knew? United had won The Double in 1997, so why not The Treble in 1999? David always set himself ambitious targets.

After a slow start to the season, United stormed ahead of Arsenal. Their team spirit was unbreakable, thanks to their amazing manager.

'It's never over until that final whistle blows!' Fergie reminded them again and again.

The players always believed they would win and whenever it looked like they might lose, someone saved the day.

There were so many matchwinners in the team – Giggsy, Scholesy, Dwight Yorke, Andy Cole, Teddy Sheringham and super sub Ole Gunnar Solskjær. Nicky got the key goal against Leeds United and even Gary got on the scoresheet against Everton.

A lot of the time, David was the one who set up the goals with his incredible crosses, free kicks and long-range passes. But in the final weeks of the season, he put his shooting boots on. With Arsenal in second place breathing down Manchester United's necks, his team needed him.

United were losing 1–0 at Wimbledon with seconds left in the first half. David crossed towards Andy, but he couldn't quite reach it. As the ball bounced around in the box, David sprinted bravely forward to score.

Goooooooooooooaaaaaaaaaalllllllllllllllllllll!!!!!!!!!!!!

It was one of his scrappiest strikes, but it was also one of his most important.

'Yes, Becks!' Dwight cheered, jumping on David's back.

United were drawing 1–1 with Aston Villa when they won a free kick. David stepped up and fooled the keeper by taking a long run-up. It looked like he was going for lots of power but, instead, he chipped the ball straight into the top corner.

Goooooooooooooooooooaaaaaaaaaaaaaaaallllllllllll llllllllllllll!!!!!!!!!!!!!!!!!!

David punched the air as he ran past the fans. 'The title is ours!' he shouted at the top of his lungs.

But on the final day of the season, United still needed to beat Tottenham to make sure. With the pressure on, they had to hold their nerve.

After twenty-five minutes, Tottenham were winning 1–0. The fans fell silent in the stands, but the players didn't panic. How many times had they fought back to win?

'Come on, we can do this!' Keano called out.

David charged around the pitch but when he got

a glorious chance to score, he fluffed it. His header flew over the bar from six yards out.

'Noooooooooo!' David cried out, putting his hands on his head.

What a miss. He had to be more composed than that.

At the end of the first half, he got a second chance. Giggsy passed to Scholesy, who passed to David. He was in space on the right, just inside the penalty area. He could cross to Dwight and Andy, but the shot looked like the better option.

'Stay calm,' David told himself. He took a touch to steady himself, then threw that left arm back and curled the ball towards the top corner. The goalkeeper got his fingertip to it, but he couldn't save it.

Goooooooooooooooooooaaaaaaaaaaaaaaaalllllllllllll llllllllllllll!!!!!!!!!!!!!!!!!!

David leapt into the air, clenching his fists at the crowd. There was no smile on his face. He was fully focused on winning.

Early in the second half, Gary played a great long-ball through to Andy Cole, who lobbed the keeper. 2–1!

Finally, David allowed himself to smile as the

whole United team celebrated together. What a moment – they were so nearly there. Eventually, the final whistle blew.

Campeones, Campeones, Olé! Olé! Olé!
United! United! United!

The players celebrated their fantastic achievement together, but they couldn't party for long. Although the Premier League season was over, *their* season wasn't. United still had two big finals to play. The Treble was on.

In a bruising FA Cup semi-final in April 1999, they had faced Arsenal. It was still 0–0 after 120 minutes of football, so the tie went to a replay. It was the last thing United needed, but in the replay at Villa Park, David gave them the lead with another brilliant long-range strike. It was his eighth goal of the season and his new favourite.

But Dennis Bergkamp made it 1–1 and the game went to extra time again. Thankfully, Giggsy saved them from a horrible penalty shoot-out. He got the ball in his own half, dribbled through the whole Arsenal defence and scored.

Despite his tired legs, David chased after his team-mate. 'Giggsy, that's the greatest goal ever!' he roared.

After the full-time whistle, the fans stormed the pitch and lifted their two wing wizards up into the air.

'The final should be a piece of cake after that!' Giggsy joked.

It wasn't, but they made sure that they got the job done and beat Newcastle 2–0. Scholesy was their Wembley hero, with an assist for Teddy and then a goal of his own. Afterwards, David and his teammates formed a big circle on the pitch and danced up and down together.

Campeones, Campeones, Olé! Olé! Olé!
United! United! United!

Their season *still* wasn't over, though, and they could *still* win The Treble. In the Champions League Final, United faced Bayern Munich. This was the trophy that David wanted most because it was the biggest club trophy in the world, and Manchester United hadn't won it since 1968.

'This is our time!' Fergie told his players before the game. 'You've done so well to get this far, but let's finish off this season in style tonight!'

David had played in lots of big matches in lots of stadiums, but nothing compared to this. Barcelona's Nou Camp was packed with 90,000 supporters and the noise was deafening. David took a deep breath and closed his eyes. He had made it to the very top of world football.

'We *can't* let the fans down!' he told Giggsy before kick-off.

They were United's key players, especially as Keano and Scholesy were both suspended. They weren't, however, in their normal positions. Giggsy was now on the right wing and David was in the middle with Nicky. David had played there before but never in a game like this – the Champions League Final.

'You can do this!' Fergie told him, looking him straight in the eyes.

But after only six minutes, United were 1–0 down. What a shocking start! Where was Keano when they needed their leader?

'Heads up, lads!' Peter Schmeichel screamed, clapping his goalkeeper gloves together. He was their captain now. 'We've got plenty of time to score!'

United were the masters of the comeback. They had done it so many times already that season, including in the semi-final against Juventus. Could they do it one more time?

David tried to curl in as many crosses as possible, but it wasn't so easy from central midfield. With time running out, corners were their best route to goal. The team was relying on David to deliver yet again.

Three added minutes. Can United score? They always score!

Even Peter was up in the box, so David had to get it right. His corner was cleared, but only as far as Giggsy. He volleyed the ball towards goal and Teddy steered it in. 1–1!

As Teddy raced away to celebrate, David jumped on his back. The noise around the Nou Camp grew even louder. The Manchester United fans had never stopped believing and neither had the players.

'We can win this now!' Giggsy shouted.

United won another corner. As David sprinted over to take it, he was buzzing with confidence. His delivery was perfect, right in the danger zone. Teddy headed the ball towards goal and Ole stuck out a leg to poke it in. 2–1!

As the Bayern players sank to their knees in despair, David jumped for joy. It was the best feeling that he had ever felt. The subs all ran over to join in the celebrations, while Peter did cartwheels around his penalty area.

It was the most amazing end to a Champions League final ever. In less than three minutes, they had gone from losing to winning. It really was the perfect end to a perfect season. Manchester United had won the Treble, capping the most successful season in the history of the football club.

'We did it!' David cheered with one arm around Gary and the other around Giggsy.

He didn't want to let go of them. They were his brothers, his best friends and his teammates. And not only were they the Champions of England, but they were now the Champions of Europe too.

Campeones, Campeones, Olé! Olé! Olé!
United! United! United!

CHAPTER 14

EURO 2000

Playing for Manchester United, David was a fans' favourite, especially now that he had helped the club to win the Treble.

Playing for England, however, in 2000, David was still Enemy Number One. The fans hadn't forgiven him for his moment of madness against Argentina at the World Cup.

'That was two years ago!' he moaned to Gary. 'Isn't it time they moved on?'

His friend laughed. 'Maybe if you do something special, they will!'

As soon as his suspension ended, David had jumped straight back into the England team. He had helped his country to qualify for Euro 2000, but he still hadn't added to that free-kick goal against Colombia at the 1998 World Cup. Gary was right – he had work to do in order to make things right.

'You mean the haircut wasn't enough?' David kidded back. His famous blonde locks were gone. With a shaved head, 'the new Becks' meant business.

Hopefully, Euro 2000 would be his time to shine. There was a relaxed atmosphere around the England training camp, and everyone was excited about the tournament ahead. Kevin Keegan was the new manager but most of the players were still the same – Tony and Sol at the back, Incey and Scholesy in the middle, Alan and Michael up front. David was the first choice on the right wing, with Steve McManaman on the left.

'How's it going at Real Madrid, Macca?' David asked Steve. He liked the idea of playing in Spain one day.

'I'm loving it!' Steve replied. 'Didn't you see my goal in the Champions League final?'

It was England's best squad for years, but it needed to be. They were up against Portugal, Germany and Romania.

'Welcome to the Group of Death, lads!' Incey joked.

It wasn't going to be easy, but England got off to a brilliant start against Portugal. In the third minute, David curled the ball in from the right and Scholesy had a free header. 1–0!

'What a cross!' Scholesy cheered, jumping into David's arms. The members of Manchester United's Class of '92 had been playing together for so long that they knew each other's movements off by heart.

Fifteen minutes later, David burst down the right wing again. This time, he chipped the ball over Scholesy's head to Steve at the back-post. 2–0!

'I've got two assists already – is that special enough yet?' he grinned at Gary.

The answer was no. The fans continued to shout horrible abuse at David.

Unfortunately, it all went downhill after that for England. Michael and Macca got injured and Luís Figo and Rui Costa led Portugal to a Manchester

United-style comeback. By half-time, it was 2–2 and by full-time, England had lost 3–2. David was devastated but he shook hands and swapped shirts with Luís.

'Well played today,' the Portuguese player said. 'I thought my right foot was dangerous but yours is *deadly*!'

Luís's kind words made David feel a little better, but it was still a bad defeat for England.

'If we don't beat Germany, that's it,' David told Victoria anxiously on the phone, 'we're out of the tournament.'

With the pressure on, however, England upped their game. Early in the second half, they won a free kick on the right.

'Take a quick one!' Gary shouted.

David shook his head. 'No, go away!'

Instead, he swung a brilliant free kick into the penalty area. The ball flew past Michael, then Scholesy, but as it bounced down, Alan was there with a diving header. 1–0!

'Great cross!' Gary cried out as he hugged David.

'Surely they'll forgive you now!'

At the final whistle, David threw his arms up in the air. What a result! England had beaten Germany in a competitive match for the first time since 1966. It was the victory that they needed, and it was all thanks, once again, to his remarkable right foot.

A draw against Romania would be enough to send them through to the quarter-finals. At half-time, England weren't drawing; they were winning! They were 2–1 up, thanks to Alan and Michael.

'You just need to keep your heads now, boys,' Keegan told them in the dressing room. 'No silly mistakes!'

Unfortunately, just after the break, England did make a silly mistake and Romania scored. Watching the ball hit the net, David's shoulders slumped. Scholesy looked over at him and his face said it all – 'Uh-oh, we're in trouble!'

England held on, however, and with seconds to go, it looked like they were through. Romania launched one last attack. As Viorel Moldovan dribbled into the penalty area, it didn't look too dangerous. They had plenty of defenders in the box, and yet Phil decided to slide in for the tackle. Instead of the ball, he kicked Moldovan's leg. Penalty!

Near the halfway line, David watched in horror and disbelief. He put his hand to his head. It was another moment of madness in a major tournament. Romania scored from the spot, and England were out of Euro 2000. What a crushing blow.

If anyone would know how Phil was feeling, it was David. He went over and put an arm around his friend. 'Hey, that wasn't your fault, okay? We weren't good enough – all of us. It's as simple as that.'

After a few days of sulking, it was time for England to move on. When one international tournament ended, another began. They now had the 2002 World Cup to qualify for.

CHAPTER 15

CAPTAIN TO THE RESCUE

6 October 2001 – Old Trafford, Manchester

The fourth official stepped forward and lifted the electronic board above his head for everyone to see – '4'.

The noise level lifted around Old Trafford. There was still time! England had four more minutes to score. David chased after every ball, desperate to save his country from an embarrassing defeat. It was like he had endless amounts of energy. Playing for England meant so much to David and, after his red card in 1998, he *had* to play at the 2002 World Cup.

His tenth match as England captain really wasn't going according to plan. All they needed was a draw against Greece to finish top of UEFA Group 9, but instead, they were losing 2–1. It was like the Romania match at Euro 2000 all over again.

'Keep going!' David shouted, urging his teammates up the field.

Everything had been going so well, ever since Peter Taylor had given him the captain's armband in November 2000. Leading his country for the first time against Italy was the proudest moment of David's life. It made him feel even more determined out on the pitch. The whole nation was relying on him.

When Sven-Göran Eriksson arrived as the new England manager, he asked David to keep wearing the armband. 'Yes, please!' he said, and the Three Lions beat Spain 3–0, then Mexico 4–0 and, best of all, Germany 5–1.

He would never forget that amazing night in Munich. From 1–0 down, England fought back brilliantly. David helped to set up three of the goals, working brilliantly with Scholesy, Michael and Steven Gerrard.

That feeling of joy and success now felt like a lifetime ago. How could England thrash Germany and yet still not qualify for the World Cup? It seemed impossible.

Nigel Martyn kicked the ball downfield to Teddy. As he jumped for the header, the Greece defender pushed him in the back. A free kick in the ninety-third minute!

The noise level lifted around Old Trafford once more. This would be David's sixth free kick of the game, and his strikes were getting closer and closer. The last one had whistled just wide of the post. Could he do better with his final attempt?

David took his time, placing the ball down carefully. He wanted to make sure that everything was perfect before he took the last kick of the match. Teddy tried to take it himself, but nothing was going to stop David.

'Trust me, I've got this,' he said firmly.

Teddy saw the focused look on his captain's face and walked away. Scholesy stood to his right in silence. He believed in his friend and teammate. He had seen David do it so many times before, especially there at his football home, Manchester United's 'Theatre of Dreams', Old Trafford.

In the stands, the fans could barely watch. Some feared the worst, but others still held out hope. If anyone could score a last-minute free kick, it was 'Becks'. The banging of a drum echoed around the stadium. Even David could hear it down on the pitch.

As he waited for the referee's whistle, David took long, deep breaths to calm his pounding heart. He needed to be as calm and composed as possible. He felt confident. 'I can do this,' he told himself. He had spent so many years practising free kicks, practising for massive moments like this.

David looked up at the goal and imagined the ball flying into the top corner of the net. He imagined the celebrations up and down the country, and the newspaper headlines – 'DAVID BECKHAM: ENGLAND HERO'. Yes, he liked the sound of that. With one kick, he could at last put his 1998 World Cup nightmare behind him.

Finally, the whistle sounded. David moved towards

the ball, slowly at first but then faster. Everyone knew his technique. He swung his left arm backwards and his remarkable right foot forwards. Bang!

The ball curled up over the wall…

'I definitely hit that well,' David thought to himself as he stood and watched. He had a good feeling about this one.

… then dipped…

'He's done it!' the fans yelled, rising to their feet. 'He's done it!'

…and landed in the top corner of the net.

Goooooooooooooooooooaaaaaaaaaaaaaaaalllllllllllll llllllllllllll!!!!!!!!!!!!!!!!!!

Captain to the rescue - David *had* done it! In that moment, the adrenaline took over. It felt even better than that Wimbledon Wonderstrike. He raced over to the fans in the corner and leapt into the air. As he landed on both feet, he threw his arms out in the air.

'We're off to the World Cup!' Emile Heskey shouted, giving him a big bear hug.

'Becks, you're a legend!' Rio Ferdinand screamed in his face.

Gary gave David the biggest hug of all. 'You know I said that you needed to do something special to win over the fans? That was it, mate! That was it!'

The dark days were over. All was forgiven.

Finally, he was back to being 'DAVID BECKHAM: ENGLAND HERO'.

CHAPTER 16

WORLD CUP 2002

With the 2002 World Cup only eight weeks away, England's captain, David was in fine form for his club. Manchester United were on their way to another Premier League title and they were through to the quarter-finals of the Champions League too.

Against Deportivo La Coruña, David got the opening goal. It was his sixteenth of the season already, and another long-range wonderstrike. That remarkable right foot of his was simply unstoppable.

'What's going on?' Scholesy said as they celebrated. 'You're scoring more than me these days!'

Sadly, David's club season was about to end. In the last minute of the game, Deportivo's striker

Diego Tristán caught him on the left foot with a bad tackle.

'Argghhhh!' David cried out.

Even though he was in so much pain, his first worry was, 'What about the World Cup?'

David needed crutches just to leave the stadium. The England fans held their breath but a week later, he was back playing against Deportivo in the second leg.

'Just see how you get on,' Ferguson told him. 'If it starts to hurt, I'll bring you off.'

It all seemed fine for the first twenty minutes, but then Aldo Duscher slid in and sent David flying. It was another reckless challenge on his left foot and this time, the pain was ten times worse.

'Argghhhh!' David cried out again, rolling around in agony.

Eventually, the team physio helped him back to his feet, but it hurt just to stand. That's when David knew that something was seriously wrong.

'It's broken, isn't it?' he asked.

The physio nodded glumly. 'I think so.'

David's heart sank. There was no way that a broken foot could heal in eight weeks. England would have to win the World Cup without him.

'Hey, you don't know that yet!' Victoria said in the ambulance on the way to the hospital. 'Let's just wait and see what the X-ray shows.'

David had never been so nervous in all his life. Finally, Victoria spoke to the doctors and brought him the news.

'Ok, so you *have* broken a bone in your foot called the metatarsal, but it looks like you should still be able to play at the World Cup,' she told him, a smile breaking out across her face.

'Really?' David replied. He was relieved but also surprised. How could a bone heal that quickly? He didn't want to get his hopes up for nothing.

'Yes, but the doctors say it's not going be easy. It sounds like a lot of hard, boring work.'

'No problem, I'll do anything I can to get fit in time!'

Day by day, the tournament got closer and closer. And day by day, David's left foot got better and better. The question on every English person's lips was: would 'Becks' be ready? The country's hopes seemed to rest on his metatarsal. It was a race against time, but like every football match he had ever played, he was determined to win.

'So, are you fit enough to play?' his manager Sven-Göran Eriksson asked a few days before the first game.

'Yes,' David replied, sounding certain. 'You try stopping me!'

With the whole nation cheering him on, he ran out as England captain against Sweden. David felt so proud to lead his country at a World Cup, especially after his injury problems. Once again, he had shown his strong character.

'Come on, boys!' he called out in the tunnel. 'Here we go!'

It was great to be back. After twenty-five minutes, David swung in one of his trademark corner-kicks and Sol powered the ball home with his head. 1–0!

Sadly, they couldn't hold on for victory. In the second-half, Niclas Alexandersson scored and the

Three Lions had to settle for a draw. That put even more pressure on England's next game – the rematch against Argentina.

David wasn't the only one who wanted revenge after the World Cup of 1998; so did Sol, Scholesy, Michael, and an entire nation of football fans. But for David, revenge would be particularly sweet.

'Let's win this, lads!' he shouted confidently.

Both teams were really fired up, but England were on top. Just before half-time, Scholesy passed to Michael inside the box. As he tricked his way past Mauricio Pochettino, the defender stuck out a leg. Penalty!

Who would take it – Michael? No, David walked straight over and grabbed the ball. This was a goal that he needed to score. He placed it down on the spot and then stepped back, trying to keep his adrenaline under control.

As David looked up, his enemy, Diego Simeone, was walking towards him. He was trying to put David off, but it wasn't going to work. Just to make sure, Nicky and Scholesy pushed the Argentinian out of the way. They always had their friend's back.

With one last deep breath, David ran forward and… swept the ball past the keeper.

Goooooooooooooooooooaaaaaaaaaaaaaaaaalllllllllllll lllllllllllllll!!!!!!!!!!!!!!!!!!!!!!

As he ran towards the fans, David lifted his shirt to his face and kissed the Three Lions.

'Come on!' he roared.

Four years of pain flashed before his eyes. He felt so emotional that he didn't know whether to laugh or cry. In the end, he did a bit of both.

That goal turned out to be the matchwinner. At the final whistle, the whole team ran over to hug David. He was definitely an England hero now.

The Three Lions roared on. With a 0–0 draw against Nigeria and a 3–0 over Denmark, they were through to the World Cup quarter-finals. Next up, Brazil and their '3 Rs' – Ronaldo, Rivaldo and Ronaldinho.

'Don't worry, Sol and I will handle those guys!' Rio reassured his teammates.

David's left foot had begun to hurt, and the

warm weather in Japan wasn't helping his tired legs. Still, the pain was all worth it to lead his country towards glory.

After twenty-three minutes, Michael gave England the lead. The team was really starting to believe that they could go all the way.

Rio and Sol kept Ronaldo quiet, but that still left Rivaldo and Ronaldinho. They scored the goals that took Brazil into the semi-finals.

David was very disappointed to get knocked out, but he was also proud of his team. England had done so well to get through 'The Group of Death' and reach the quarter-finals. David was also proud of himself. Not only had he recovered from injury just in time, but he had also redeemed himself against Argentina.

The England team's future looked bright. David couldn't wait for his next international adventures – Euro 2004 and then the 2006 World Cup.

CHAPTER 17

LEAVING OLD TRAFFORD

David returned to Manchester United, feeling as excited as ever about winning trophies. Even after five Premier League titles, two FA Cups and one Champions League trophy, he still wanted more.

David still had that incredible hunger that Alex Ferguson had spotted so many years ago. The Manchester United manager wasn't quite so sure, however. He noticed that David's dyed blonde hair was back, and that he had so many celebrity commitments. Was David *really* focused on football? Fergie pushed his players very hard. He expected 100 per cent effort from all of them, but especially from his 'Fledglings' like David.

'What more can I do to show him?' David asked Gary. 'We're top of the Premier League and we're still in the Champions League!'

'Just keep playing well and everything will soon go back to normal,' his friend advised.

In the Champions League quarter-final, United were up against the 'Galácticos' of Real Madrid – Raúl, Roberto Carlos, Luís Figo, Zinedine Zidane and Ronaldo. It was already an amazing team but every summer, they signed a new superstar. Rumours were spreading that David would be next.

'No way!' he protested. 'I'm not going anywhere. I love it here in Manchester.'

In the first leg at Real Madrid's Bernabéu stadium, the Galácticos outplayed United. Luís got one goal and Raúl got two in a 3–1 win.

'Come on, we can still turn things around at Old Trafford,' David told his teammates on the way back to England.

United never gave up. They always believed that they could win, no matter what. That's what made them such a successful team – Gary, Phil, Keano,

Nicky, David, Giggsy and Scholesy.

On the day of the second leg, however, Fergie called David into his office. 'I'm afraid that you're not starting tonight. You'll be on the bench.'

He couldn't believe it. Ahead of the biggest game of the season, he had been dropped. That hurt so much. David left Fergie's office without saying a word.

'That's it!' he muttered to himself as he stormed down the corridor.

For sixty minutes, David sat and watched Ronaldo tear United apart with an amazing hat-trick. It was awful to feel so helpless on the bench. David was itching to get out there and prove his manager wrong. Finally, he got his chance. United needed three goals – and quickly.

Straight away, David whipped in a brilliant cross for Ole Gunnar, but he headed just wide.

'Unlucky!' David clapped, urging his team to keep going.

United won a free kick just outside the Real Madrid penalty area. There was only one remarkable right foot that could take it, and there was only one place where the ball could end up. Bang!

Gooooooooooooooooooooaaaaaaaaaaaaaaaaalllllllllllllllllllllllllll!!!!!!!!!!!!!!!!!!!!

David punched the air and high-fived Giggsy. Only two more goals to go! In the middle of the match, Roberto Carlos called out to him, 'So, are you coming to play for us?'

David didn't reply. He was too busy trying to keep United in the Champions League. Ruud van Nistelrooy dribbled towards goal. His shot was saved but David slid in to score his second of the night.

Gooooooooooooooooooooaaaaaaaaaaaaaaaaalllllllllllllllllllllllllll!!!!!!!!!!!!!!!!!!!!

Only one more goal to go! In stoppage time, United won another free kick just outside the Real Madrid penalty area. Could David rescue his team with a hat-trick? His strike flew over the wall, towards the top corner... but just over the crossbar.

So close! United were out, but David felt proud of his own performance. He had proved his dedication to the club. As he walked around the pitch, the fans gave him a standing ovation.

'Don't leave, Becks!' they shouted.

After that match, there were more and more stories about David moving to Real Madrid. It felt nice to be wanted by such a top club.

'It would be pretty cool to play with Zidane and Ronaldo...' he started thinking.

Out on the pitch, David finished the 2002–03 season in style. He scored against Charlton and Everton, as United sealed yet another league title. He was right at the heart of the team's celebrations, with one arm around Scholesy and the other around Juan Sebastián Verón.

'I love it here,' David thought to himself happily that day. 'No, I'm not going anywhere!'

In the end, however, it wasn't David's decision. During the summer, United accepted offers from Barcelona and Real Madrid.

David couldn't believe it. Was he really leaving Old Trafford after twelve incredible years? It was his home, the place where he had developed as a footballer and as a person. At Manchester United, his teammates weren't just teammates. Gary, Phil, Nicky, Scholesy and Giggsy were his best friends, his brothers. David had grown up with them.

And what about his family? It was a huge decision for all of them. Could he make Victoria and their sons move to Spain? It would be a new life in a new country, with a new language and a new culture.

'We'll support you, whatever you choose to do,' his wife reassured him.

Well, if David was going to leave Manchester United, it could only be to join one club – Real Madrid. He loved playing at the Bernabéu, and he loved the stylish football that the Galácticos played. He spoke to their president on the phone.

'I think you are one of the best footballers in the world,' Florentino Pérez told him, 'and we believe that you can make our team even better.'

A few days later, the deal was done. David and his family were off on an exciting Spanish adventure. Before he could get down to football, however, he had to choose a shirt number. Raúl wore his favourite Number 7, Ronaldo wore Number 9 and

Luís wore Number 10. What about 8 or 11?

'No, I'll take Number Twenty-Three,' David decided. That was the number that his basketball hero Michael Jordan had worn for the Chicago Bulls.

Dressed in a pale blue suit, David smiled for the cameras and held up the famous white Real Madrid shirt with '23 BECKHAM' on the back. He was now a Galáctico, playing for the Spanish champions. It was yet another dream come true.

'Hala Madrid!' David cheered.

CHAPTER 18

LIFE AS A GALÁCTICO

As David prepared for his first training session at Real Madrid, he couldn't help missing Manchester United. His life had been so easy there, playing with the same familiar players and managed by the same familiar manager.

Now, everything was different and daunting. He was about to meet his new teammates and what if they didn't like him? What if he didn't fit in?

David arrived early and sat in the dressing room, waiting nervously. He didn't want to steal anyone's seat, so he sat on the physio's bed instead.

Luís was the first to arrive.

'Hola, how are you?' he asked, with a friendly smile.

David's Spanish was poor, and his Portuguese was even worse, so he was relieved to hear Luis' excellent English.

The Galácticos entered one by one, each giving him a warm welcome.

'I knew you'd be here soon!' Roberto Carlos laughed.

'As soon as Macca leaves, another Englishman arrives!' Zinedine joked.

'Here you go,' Raúl smiled, handing David two sheets of paper. 'Your survival kit!'

It was a list of Spanish football phrases. 'Thanks, you're a lifesaver!' David replied.

David couldn't wait to get started at Real Madrid. It was an amazing opportunity and a real challenge too. Off the pitch, the Galácticos were a relaxed bunch but on it, they were hard-working professionals. David had lots to learn to earn his place amongst them.

The season started with the Spanish Super Cup Final against Mallorca. After a 2–1 away defeat, Real needed a big win in David's home debut. In front of the roaring Bernabéu crowd, the superstars came alive.

Roberto Carlos crossed to Raúl. 1–0!

Luís passed to Ronaldo. 2–0!

David celebrated both goals with his teammates, but he was desperate to get in on the act. He needed a goal or an assist. He struck a fierce free kick, but it curled just over the crossbar.

'Unlucky!' Roberto Carlos said, giving him a high-five. 'Keep going!'

In the second half, Ronaldo won the ball on the left wing. As he looked up, he spotted David in space in the middle. His cross was perfect. As the goalkeeper rushed out towards him, David kept his eyes on the ball and headed it calmly into the empty net.

Gooooooooooooooooooooaaaaaaaaaaaaaaaaalllllllllllll llllllllllllll!!!!!!!!!!!!!!!!!!!

David jumped up and punched the air. He was off the mark in a Real Madrid shirt! As he raised his arms up, the fans cheered. He was officially a Galáctico now.

'Thanks mate!' David shouted to Ronaldo as they hugged.

His La Liga debut was even better. After two minutes, Ronaldo played a one-two with Raúl and then crossed to the back post. David raced in from the right wing to smash the ball into the net.

Goooooooooooooooooooaaaaaaaaaaaaaaaalllllllllllll llllllllllllll!!!!!!!!!!!!!!!!!!!

This time, he jumped into Ronaldo's arms. 'You're the best!' he cheered.

All that was missing now was one of David's famous free kicks. The fans were desperate to see one. Against Málaga, Roberto Carlos stood ready to run up and strike it but at the last moment, he moved away. It was David's turn! The goalkeeper moved to his left, but David put so much curl on the shot that it ended up in the opposite corner.

Goooooooooooooooooooaaaaaaaaaaaaaaaalllllllllllll llllllllllllll!!!!!!!!!!!!!!!!!!!

Even David was surprised by how quickly he had settled in at Real Madrid. After only a month, he was already a key part of the team. With so many superstars on the pitch together, someone had to track back and help the defence. David was happy to be that someone. He had the energy and work rate to get up and down the pitch all game long.

'Finally, a Galáctico who doesn't just attack, attack, attack!' their goalkeeper Iker Casillas joked.

David still had that remarkable right foot, though. At times, it was like a magic wand.

Against Valladolid, he played a spectacular long pass from right to left for Zinedine to volley into the net. 4–0!

Against local rivals Atlético Madrid, he played an even more spectacular long pass for Raúl to head the ball over the goalkeeper. 2–0!

Everything was going so well. By March, Real Madrid were top of the Spanish league and into the Spanish Cup final. David couldn't wait to win more trophies.

In the final against Real Zaragoza, he scored another incredible free kick to give his team the lead. But just as the supporters got ready to party, their team collapsed in spectacular style; Real Madrid lost 3–2 in extra time.

'How did we let that happen?' David groaned, staring down at the grass beneath his feet. He hated losing so much, especially in finals.

It was a huge blow for the Galácticos and things soon got even worse. Back in the league, they lost six out of their last seven matches and ended up down in fourth place.

The fans were furious. With so much talent in the team, why weren't Real Madrid winning everything?

'Get ready for some changes this summer,' Roberto Carlos warned David.

During his twelve years at Manchester United, David had only ever played under one manager – Fergie. He was always there, and everyone trusted him.

At Real Madrid, however, they fired managers all the time. There was so much pressure to be successful straight away. During the 2004–05 season alone, David had three different bosses.

'This is ridiculous!' he complained to Michael

Owen, who had just joined him in Madrid. 'How are we supposed to win things with all this chaos around us?'

For the next two seasons in a row, Real Madrid finished second behind Barcelona. It was very frustrating to get so close to the title, and to lose out to their biggest rivals. Sometimes, the Galácticos were unstoppable but sometimes, they fell apart.

David, however, refused to give up. As Fergie had always taught him, it wasn't over until the final whistle blew. After winning so many trophies in England, David couldn't leave Spain empty-handed.

'I won't stop until we win the league!' he promised his teammates.

CHAPTER 19

PORTUGAL PAIN
PART I

David had a good feeling about Euro 2004. Looking around at all the talent in the squad, he truly believed that he could be the England captain who would finally end the thirty-eight years of hurt since 1966. How amazing would that be!

The Golden Generation was at its peak. In defence, Gary and Sol were joined by John Terry and Ashley Cole. In midfield, David and Scholesy were joined by Steven Gerrard and Frank Lampard. And in attack, Michael was joined by an eighteen-year-old wonderkid called Wayne Rooney.

'This is our best chance yet!' David kept telling his teammates. 'We just have to believe!'

That was especially important in the first match

against Zinedine's France, the winners of Euro 2000.

As he led the team out onto the pitch in Portugal, David could see the calm confidence on everyone's faces. They could beat France; they could beat anyone!

Late in the first half, England won a free kick on the right. David was ready to take it with his remarkable right foot. The ball fizzed in towards Frank and he glanced it into the top corner. 1–0!

'Get in!' David roared, punching the air.

In the second half, he played a great pass upfield to Wayne, who dribbled all the way into the box before a defender hacked him down. Penalty!

Once more, David was ready to take it with his remarkable right foot. England wouldn't get a better chance to go 2–0 up. He just had to beat his old Manchester teammate, Fabien Barthez.

David struck the ball well and right towards the corner but Barthez had guessed the right way. He flung himself across the goal. Saved!

Never mind, there was no time for David to feel sorry for himself. He chased back to defend, calling out, 'Come on boys, we're still 1–0 up!'

England held on bravely until the ninetieth minute when France won a free kick and Zinedine stepped up to take it. David jumped up in the wall, but the ball curved round them and into the bottom corner. 1–1! Zinedine's was a strike that even he would be proud of.

'Never mind, lads,' David shouted, trying to lift the spirits around him. 'A draw will do – focus!'

But in the final seconds, Steven played a back pass without looking behind him. Thierry Henry was on to it in a flash and he got to the ball just before the sliding goalkeeper. Penalty! Zinedine sent David James the wrong way, and it was 2–1 to France!

The England players stood there in shock. How had they lost that? David couldn't stop thinking about his spot-kick miss. If it had gone in, they would have won for sure.

'No mate, that wasn't a bad penalty,' Scholesy told him. 'It was a great save.'

It was time to move on. David was the captain and he had to make his teammates believe again.

'For ninety minutes, we were brilliant,' he told

them. 'If we keep playing like that, we'll win our next two matches. Forget about those last three minutes – we're better than that!'

England went on to beat Switzerland and Croatia in style, with Wayne scoring four goals. The team was in great form, so why couldn't they go all the way and win Euro 2004?

'Let's take one game at a time,' Gary warned from experience. 'This is knockout football now – any mistakes will cost us big time.'

Those were wise words, especially as England were about to play the hosts of the tournament in the quarter-finals. As well as having the home crowd behind them, Portugal also had lots of dangerous attackers, like David's Real Madrid teammate, Luís Figo, and his replacement at Manchester United, Cristiano Ronaldo.

None of that fazed England, though. Michael scored in only the third minute of the match. What a perfect start!

'Right, focus!' Gary called out from the back.

The Three Lions battled brilliantly, even when Wayne limped off with an injury. The semi-finals were in touching distance.

'Last push now, lads!' David shouted, shaking out his tired legs. 'Keep going!'

But with ten minutes to go, Hélder Postiga scored to make it 1–1. After thirty minutes of extra-time, that became 2–2. It was time for penalties.

To atone for his infamous absence from the penalty shootout against Argentina at the World Cup in 1998, David went first for England. As captain, he had to stand up and take responsibility.

'I've got this,' he told his manager confidently.

As David placed the ball down on the spot, he felt sure that he would score. But as he ran up to kick it, his left foot slipped on the grass. He was off balance and his right foot sliced the shot horribly. The ball sailed high over the crossbar.

'Nooooooooo!' David screamed, staring down at the pitch for answers. What had just happened? Why wasn't the ball in the back of the net? His remarkable right foot had failed.

David's heart sank. He had worked so hard to turn things around for his country, from villain in 1998 to hero in 2002. Now, he was England's villain once more.

Before Michael took the next penalty, he stamped down the turf around the spot. England couldn't afford to miss another one. Thankfully, he scored, and so did Frank, and so did John Terry, Owen Hargreaves and Ashley Cole. The shoot-out went to sudden death.

On the halfway line, David could hardly watch as Darius Vassell made the long walk forward. The Portugal goalkeeper, Ricardo, had taken his gloves off. He was *that* confident that he was going to save Darius' penalty, and he did. Ricardo then took Portugal's winning penalty himself.

David was devastated but he didn't forget his captain's role. Just as he had with Phil at Euro 2000, he went over and put his arm around Darius.

'Hey, you did everything you could tonight. Be proud. We'll get another chance, I promise!'

David's international dreams now rested on the 2006 World Cup. England certainly had the talent to win it, but did they have the nerve? Only time would tell.

CHAPTER 20

PORTUGAL PAIN PART II

With two wins and a draw, England got off to a strong start at the 2006 World Cup in Germany, and qualified for the knockout stage. The team spirit was sky high in the squad. They were determined to stay strong and conquer, despite the injuries.

Just as Wayne returned, Michael was stretchered off. But fear not! With David delivering incredible crosses to 'Two Metre' Peter Crouch, the dream was still alive.

Next up was Ecuador. They weren't as famous as their South American rivals Brazil and Argentina, but they still had plenty of skill and speed. At half-time, England were lucky to still be level at 0–0.

'Come on lads, wake up!' David shouted in the dressing room.

With Michael and Scholesy missing, he was now their most experienced attacker, as well as their captain. Wayne still wasn't 100 per cent fit, and Steven and Frank were struggling to score. That left David and his remarkable right foot. What could he do to lead England to the World Cup quarter-finals again?

'What's going on with your free kicks, Becks?' Wayne had been teasing him in training. 'They've been rubbish so far! Are you losing your golden touch?'

His first attempt flew harmlessly wide, but that didn't get David down. He just hoped that he would get a second chance. When it arrived, he knew exactly what he had to do.

As he waited for the whistle, lots of England memories flooded through his head:

The free kick against Colombia at the 1998 World Cup, his first ever international goal.

The free kick against Greece to save the day for his country.

The successful penalty against Argentina at the 2002 World Cup.

The missed penalties against France and Portugal at Euro 2004.

But what about the 2006 World Cup? David was determined to make it a happy memory for himself and for the millions of England fans watching.

From wide on the left, he had two options:

1) Curl a cross into the penalty area

2) Curl a shot into the top corner.

Option 1 was what everyone was expecting – the England players in the box, the England supporters in the stadium, and, most importantly, the Ecuador goalkeeper.

With that thought in his head, David went for Option 2 instead. He was desperate to score a goal for his country and he might not get a better chance.

'Get one for me today,' his Real Madrid teammate Roberto Carlos had texted him earlier that day.

The angle wasn't easy, but David's accuracy was amazing. The ball clipped the post on its way into the net.

Goooooooooooooooooooooaaaaaaaaaaaaaaaalllllllllllllll llllllllllllll!!!!!!!!!!!!!!!!!!!

'YES!' David cried out as his teammates rushed over to him. What a crucial strike! He was now the first England player in history to score in three different World Cups.

'You've still got it, Becks!' Wayne cheered, looking mightily relieved.

In the crowd, Victoria jumped for joy. Her husband was the national hero once again.

England were through to the World Cup quarter-finals again, but they had to work to do. If they played that badly again against Portugal, Luís and Cristiano would hammer them.

'We've got to keep our heads,' David told the players, 'but let's show some passion out there. This is our chance for revenge!'

In the end, David only lasted fifty minutes in the harsh sun. After his heroics against Ecuador, he was struggling with illness and injury. He was desperate to carry on for his country, but his ankle was getting more and more painful.

'Good luck, go use your speed!' he told his replacement, Aaron Lennon.

From the bench, David watched another England moment of madness. Wayne was getting more and more frustrated with Portugal's tough tackling.

'Come on, ref!' he screamed. 'They're fouling me every time!

Wayne needed to calm down, but David wasn't there on the pitch to look after him anymore. After one more heavy challenge, the striker lost his temper. Red card!

'Here we go again,' David thought to himself. First Argentina, and now Portugal.

Again, England battled on bravely. Again, the match went to penalties, and again, England lost.

'We're cursed,' David muttered, with his head in his hands.

After a few minutes, he picked himself up and went back onto the pitch to thank the fans for all their support.

Was David saying goodbye? He wasn't sure, but he was sure about one thing:

'It has been an honour to captain my country for fifty-eight games, but I feel the time is right to pass on the armband,' he announced sadly.

Was that the end of David's World Cup dream? Not necessarily. At the next tournament in 2010, he would be thirty-five but if he was fit enough and his country needed him, he would never say no to England.

CHAPTER 21

OFF TO AMERICA

During the 2006–07 season at Real Madrid, David started thinking about his future. He wasn't playing as many games under new manager Fabio Capello, and his contract would soon run out. So, what next? At thirty-one years of age, David still had plenty of time left for one more football adventure.

'Where do you want to go?' his agent asked him. 'Back to England?'

David shook his head. He loved Manchester United too much to play for one of their Premier League rivals.

'Have you thought about America? Major League Soccer would love to have a player like you, especially at your age.'

In the past, fading superstars had often moved to the USA for one final season. The American fans loved to see famous faces but what they really wanted was top players in their prime. David fitted that description perfectly.

'You could help to change the image of the MLS and turn it into a great league,' his agent continued. 'Who knows, maybe one day you could even have your own club!'

David loved that idea. Los Angeles was one of his favourite places in the world and their team, the LA Galaxy, soon made him an offer that he couldn't refuse.

'I guess a Galáctico has to join the Galaxy!' he laughed.

At the end of the season, David would be off to America. First, however, he put all of his effort into winning the Spanish League with Real Madrid. He fought his way back into the starting line-up and set up lots of important goals. Finally, after years of trying, Real Madrid beat their big rivals Barcelona to the title.

Campeones, Campeones, Olé! Olé! Olé!

David was delighted with his winners' medal. It was the perfect way to end four fantastic years as a Galáctico.

'Adiós!' he waved to the amazing Real Madrid fans.

'Hello!' he waved to the people of America. They were very excited about his arrival. 'Becks' was going to take the MLS to the next level.

Back home, however, people criticised David's move:

'He's only going for the money. Why else would you go and play "soccer" out there?'

'Surely, that's the end of his England career? The MLS is rubbish!'

As always, David just ignored the cruel comments. They weren't true. He wasn't in LA for a beach holiday. He was fully focused on playing football and proving people wrong about American 'soccer'.

'And there's no reason why I can't keep representing my country!' he argued passionately.

David's first few seasons with the Galaxy weren't

as successful as he'd hoped. Despite scoring some trademark free-kicks and a Wimbledon-esque wonderstrike, he couldn't lead the team to MLS glory. He was selling lots of tickets and shirts, but he wasn't lifting trophies.

'It's great that more people are watching us,' he told his new manager Bruce Arena, 'but I want them to watch us *win*!'

With David's help, the Galaxy got better and better. In 2009, they lost to Real Salt Lake on penalties in the MLS Cup Final. It was a cruel way to lose but David stayed positive.

'Heads up, guys, we're getting closer!'

By 2011, they had one of the best attacks in the league. American star Landon Donovan and Irish star Robbie Keane were the strikers, with David creating magic in central midfield. The fans called them 'The LA Power Trio'.

In the quarter-finals of the MLS Cup, they faced Thierry Henry's New York Red Bulls. It was a battle of the former Premier League stars.

'It's like Manchester United vs Arsenal all over

again!' they joked before kick-off.

Once the match started, however, David was determined to come out on top. He set up all three goals with his remarkable right foot.

'Come on, this is our year!' he cheered confidently.

Thirty thousand fans filled the stadium in California to watch David and co take on the Houston Dynamo in the 2011 MLS Cup Final. After a frustrating first half, the Galaxy's stars came out to shine. David flicked a header on to Robbie, who passed through to Landon, who lifted his shot over the keeper. 1–0!

A smile of joy and relief spread across David's face. At the final whistle, Landon jumped into his arms.

'We've done it!' they screamed together.

After five years of trying, David had finally achieved his American Dream. He was an MLS champion. As he lifted the cup above his head, confetti filled the air and the crowd roared. David's sons Brooklyn, Romeo and Cruz joined him on the pitch, all wearing LA Galaxy scarves.

'Well done, Dad!' they cheered. It was a proud moment for the whole family.

David had only signed a five-year contract at the Galaxy, and those five years were now up. What next? He decided to stay in Los Angeles for another season.

'I want to win back-to-back MLS Cups!' David told the media.

And that's exactly what he did. For the 2012 final, the Galaxy were back at the same stadium against the same opponents, the Houston Dynamo. Would the LA Power Trio come out on top again?

David played a beautiful long ball to Robbie, who passed across to Landon in the penalty area, who... shot wide! All three of the Galaxy stars stood with their hands on their heads. They couldn't believe they weren't 1–0 up. By half-time, however, they were 1–0 *down*.

'Come on, we just need to take one of our chances,' David told his teammates.

He was desperate to be the Galaxy hero in his last game for the club, but in the end, it was Landon and

Robbie who scored the crucial goals. As long as his team won, David didn't mind.

'Back-to-back, baby!' Landon laughed.

After eighty-nine minutes, David was substituted and the fans all stood up to clap their superstar. When he first arrived in LA, he had promised them glory and he hadn't let them down.

David had left Real Madrid with a trophy and now he was leaving the LA Galaxy with a trophy too. It felt like the perfect way to end his American adventure. His final farewell, however, was even more perfect.

The US President invited the whole team to the White House for a special celebration. It was a huge honour.

'David, half of your teammates could be your kids,' Barack Obama joked during his speech. 'We're getting old, though you're holding up better than me!'

CHAPTER 22

MILAN AND PARIS

Even during his American adventure, David kept
in touch with Europe's top clubs. The MLS season
finished in December each year, so he needed to
keep himself fit during the break leading up to the
Spring.

'If I'm going to make the 2010 World Cup squad,'
David argued, 'I can't just sit around on the beach!'

In January 2009, he joined Italian giants AC Milan
on loan. It was an amazing opportunity to play with
lots of the best players in the world – Paolo Maldini,
Clarence Seedorf, Kaká, Andrea Pirlo, Andriy
Shevchenko, Ronaldinho… the list went on and on.

AC Milan were the 'Galácticos' of Italy, which

suited David perfectly. After his days at Real Madrid, he was used to playing in a team full of superstars.

'Don't worry, you just focus on your skills!' he joked with Ronaldinho. 'I'll do all the running for you!'

David wasn't as quick as he used to be, but in other ways, he had improved over the years. Rather than playing on the right wing, he often now played in central midfield. Experience had taught him to read the game well and spot the space before anyone else. He was a more intelligent footballer now.

Against Bologna, David got the ball on the right side of the penalty area. He faked to cross like normal but instead, he beat the keeper at his near post.

Goooooooooooooooooooaaaaaaaaaaaaaaaaalllllllllllll lllllllllllll!!!!!!!!!!!!!!!!!!

'Mate, that was clever!' Clarence shouted.

In the next match against Genoa, AC Milan won a free-kick wide on the left. 'I've got this one,' David told Andrea confidently. It was time to show that his remarkable right foot was still as deadly as ever. David faked to cross the ball into the box but again, he curled it in at the near post instead.

Goooooooooooooooooooaaaaaaaaaaaaaaaalllllllllllll llllllllllllll!!!!!!!!!!!!!!!!!!!!!

David hoped that the England manager, Fabio Capello, was watching. His AC Milan manager certainly was.

'You're making an enormous difference here!' Carlo Ancelotti said happily. 'How long can you stay?'

In the end, David stayed until the summer, and he returned the next year too. He loved Italian life and his top teammates. He even got to play at Old Trafford again, when AC Milan took on his beloved old club in the Champions League.

'Welcome home, Becks!' Scholesy said with a smile.

It was an incredible feeling to run on to his favourite pitch once more and hear the Manchester United fans chanting his name. At the end, David picked up a club scarf and wrapped it around his neck. He would always be a Red Devil at heart – and, of course, a proud Englishman. Sadly, however, David missed the 2010 World Cup through injury. That spelt the end of his international career.

Through the highs and the lows, it had always

been a pleasure and an honour to represent England. He had made 115 appearances for his country, 58 of those as the captain. He had played at three World Cups, scoring in each of them. A total of 17 goals in 14 years didn't sound like much, but each strike was so important, none more so than that free kick against Greece in 2001.

'We'll miss you,' the new national team captain, Steven Gerrard, told him. 'The World Cup won't be the same without you!'

David's club career wasn't quite over yet, though. After returning to the LA Galaxy and ending his American adventure in style, he accepted one last challenge at Paris Saint-Germain in France.

'Come to PSG, we need your experience!' his old AC Milan manager Ancelotti persuaded him.

When it came to football, David couldn't say no. It wasn't about the money at all. In fact, he donated all of his salary to children's charities. No, for David, it was all about his love for the beautiful game.

'Let's do this!' he said, feeling just as excited as when he played his first match for Manchester

United twenty years earlier.

When David arrived, PSG were already top of the table. Did they really need him? Yes! His new teammates welcomed him immediately, even star striker Zlatan Ibrahimović.

'Great, now that you're here, maybe the paparazzi will leave me in peace!' he joked.

David and Zlatan quickly became best mates, both on and off the pitch. With his amazing long passes and crosses, David helped to set up lots of goals for his Swedish friend.

'Are you sure you want to retire at the end of this season?' Zlatan asked as they hugged. 'We've got a great connection!'

It was very tempting to carry on at PSG, but David had already made his decision. After winning the league in England, Spain, the USA and now France, it was time to hang up his boots.

'I know I don't look it, Zlat, but I'm thirty-eight!'

Ancelotti made David captain for his final home game against Brest. It was a very emotional day with his family there watching. There was time for him to set up one last goal before he left the field for good. As he hugged his teammates one by one, the tears streamed down his face.

On the big screens, the message was short and sweet: 'THANK YOU, DAVID'.

In the stands, the PSG fans stood to clap and cheer their English star. He had only been at the club for five months, but he had left his mark.

David Beckham! David Beckham! David Beckham!

He was really going to miss that incredible feeling of love and support. Whether he was playing for Manchester United, England, Real Madrid, LA Galaxy, AC Milan or PSG, David had always given 100 per cent out on the pitch.

Even during the most difficult moments of his career – getting sent off against Argentina in 1998, leaving Old Trafford in 2003 – he had never given up. That's why fans around the world loved David. That, and of course, his remarkable right foot.

ENGLAND'S NEXT SUPERSTAR

2005

'Welcome!' David announced to a group of sixteen boys and girls. He was there in East London to launch his brand new football academy. 'Today, we're going to practise some of my favourite skills.'

With their hero watching and cameras everywhere, none of the kids wanted to make any silly mistakes as they dribbled up and down. One boy, however, was particularly eager to impress.

'That's it, great work everyone!' David called out.

At the end of the day, he shook each of them by the hand and chatted with them. When it was the boy's turn, he was too nervous to speak.

'Well done today. Are you one of the lads from Chingford?' David asked. He had invited a group from his old secondary school.

The boy nodded. 'A-and I play for Ridgeway Rovers too.'

David smiled. 'Great club. So what's next? What's your dream?'

'I want to play for England at Wembley!'

'Good choice, it's the best feeling in the world. If you keep working hard, you can do it. What's your name, kid? I'll have to remember you for the future!'

'Harry,' the boy replied, growing in confidence. 'Harry Kane.'

Turn the page for a sneak preview
of another brilliant Ultimate Football Heroes
story – KANE by Matt and Tom Oldfield. . .

KANE

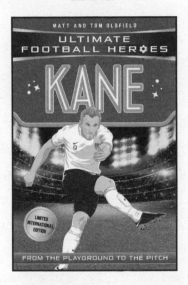

Available now!

CHAPTER 1

ENGLAND HERO

Thursday, 5 October 2017

In the Wembley tunnel, Harry closed his eyes and soaked up the amazing atmosphere. He was back at the home of football, the stadium where he had first achieved his childhood dream of playing for England. 19 March 2015, England vs Lithuania – he remembered that game like it was yesterday. He had scored that day and now, with England facing Slovenia, he needed to do it again. As England's captain and Number 9, it was his job to shoot them to the 2018 World Cup.

'Come on, lads!' Harry called out to his teammates behind him, friends like Joe Hart, Kyle Walker and Eric Dier. It was a real honour to be their leader.

With a victory over Slovenia, they would all be on their way to the biggest tournament of their lives in Russia.

Harry looked down at the young mascot by his side and smiled at him. 'Right, let's do this!'

As the two of them led the England team out on to the pitch, the fans clapped and cheered. Harry didn't look up at the thousands of faces and flags; instead, he looked down at the grass in front of him. He was totally focused on his task: scoring goals and beating Slovenia.

'If you get a chance, test the keeper,' Harry said to his partners in attack, Raheem Sterling and Marcus Rashford, before kick-off. 'I'll be there for the rebound!'

Harry's new Premiership season with Tottenham Hotspur had not begun well in August, but by September he was back to his lethal best. That month alone, he scored an incredible 13 goals, including two goals for England against Malta. He could score every type of goal – tap-ins, headers, one-on-ones, long-range shots, penalties, even free kicks.

That's what made him such a dangerous striker.

With Slovenia defending well, Harry didn't get many chances in the first half. He got in good positions but the final ball never arrived.

'There's no need to panic yet,' Harry told his teammates in the dressing room. He really didn't want a repeat of England's terrible performance against Iceland at Euro 2016. That match still haunted him. 'We're good enough to win this by playing our natural game. Be patient!'

As Ryan Bertrand dribbled down the left wing, Harry sprinted towards the six-yard box. Ryan's cross didn't reach him but the ball fell to Raheem instead. His shot was going in until a defender deflected it wide.

'Unlucky!' Harry shouted, putting his hands on his head. 'Keep going, we're going to score!'

Without this kind of strong self-belief, Harry would never have made it to the top of European football. There had been lots of setbacks along the way: rejections, disappointments and bad form. But every time, Harry bounced back with crucial goals at crucial moments. That's what made him such a superstar.

A matter of seconds later, a rebound fell to him on the edge of the penalty area. Surely, this was his moment. He pulled back his left foot and curled a powerful shot towards the bottom corner. The fans were already up on their feet, ready to celebrate. Harry never missed... but this time he did. The ball flew just wide of the post. Harry couldn't believe it. He looked up at the sky and sighed.

On the sideline, England manager Gareth Southgate cheered his team on. 'That's much better – the goal is coming, lads!'

But after ninety minutes, the goal still hadn't come. The fourth official raised his board: eight minutes of injury time.

'It's not over yet, boys!' Harry shouted, to inspire his teammates.

The Slovenian goalkeeper tried to throw the ball out to his left-back but Kyle got there first. Straight away, Harry was on the move from the back post to the front post. After playing together for years at

Tottenham, they knew how to score great goals.

As Kyle crossed it in, Harry used his burst of speed to get in front of the centre-back. Again, the England supporters stood and waited anxiously. The ball was perfect and Harry stretched out his long right leg to meet it. The keeper got a touch on his shot but he couldn't keep it out.

GOAL!

He had done it! Joy, relief, pride – Harry felt every emotion as he ran towards the fans. This time, he hadn't let them down. He held up the Three Lions on his shirt and screamed until his throat got sore.

'Captain to the rescue!' Kyle laughed as they hugged by the corner flag.

'No, it was all thanks to you!' Harry replied.

At the final whistle, he threw his arms up in the air. It was a phenomenal feeling to qualify for the 2018 World Cup. He couldn't wait to lead England to glory.

'We are off to Russia!' a voice shouted over the loudspeakers and the whole stadium cheered.

It was yet another moment that Harry would

never forget. Against the odds, he was making his childhood dreams come true. He was the star striker for Tottenham, the club that he had supported all his life. And now, like his hero David Beckham, he was the captain of England.

Harry had never given up, even when it looked like he wouldn't make it as a professional footballer. With the support of his family and his coaches, and lots of hard work and dedication, he had proved everyone wrong to become a world-class goal machine.

It had been an incredible journey from Walthamstow to Wembley, and Harry was only just getting started.

DAVID BECKHAM HONOURS

Manchester United

🏆 FA Youth Cup: 1992

🏆 Premier League: 1995–96, 1996–97, 1998–99, 1999–2000, 2000–01, 2002–03

🏆 FA Cup: 1995–96, 1998–99

🏆 UEFA Champions League: 1998–99

Real Madrid

🏆 Liga: 2006–07

🏆 LA Galaxy

🏆 MLS Cup: 2011, 2012

PSG

🏆 Ligue 1: 2012–13

Individual

🏆 PFA Young Player of the Year: 1996–97

🏆 Premier League PFA Team of the Year: 1996–97, 1997–98, 1998–99, 1999–2000

🏆 Premier League leader in assists: 1997–98, 1999–2000, 2000–01

🏆 UEFA Club Footballer of the Year: 1998–99

🏆 Ballon d'Or – Runner-up: 1999

🏆 UEFA Team of the Year: 2001, 2003

🏆 England Player of the Year: 2003

🏆 Real Madrid Player of the Year: 2005–06

🏆 MLS Comeback Player of the Year Award: 2011

BECKHAM

7, 23 32

THE FACTS

NAME: David Robert Joseph Beckham

DATE OF BIRTH: 2 May 1975

AGE: 42

PLACE OF BIRTH: Leytonstone

NATIONALITY: English

BEST FRIEND: Gary Neville

CURRENT CLUB: Manchester United, Real Madrid, LA Galaxy, AC Milan, PSG

POSITION: RM

THE STATS

Height (cm):	183
Club appearances:	719
Club goals:	129
Club trophies:	18
International appearances:	115
International goals:	17
International trophies:	0
Ballon d'Ors:	0

★ ★ ★ **HERO RATING: 89** ★ ★ ★

GREATEST MOMENTS

Type and search the web links to see the magic for yourself!

17 AUGUST 1996, WIMBLEDON 0-3 MANCHESTER UNITED

https://www.youtube.com/watch?v=u4tVnpwp8d4

David was already a famous footballer in England, but this Wimbledon Wonderstrike turned him into an international superstar. In the first match of the Premier League season, David got the ball just inside his own half and decided to take a long-range shot. The incredible strike flew over the keeper's head and into the net. Even Eric Cantona said, 'What a goal!'

26 JUNE 1998, COLOMBIA 0-2 ENGLAND

https://www.youtube.com/watch?v=6b6h5AfGvk0

Nearly two years after his England debut, David was still waiting for his first international goal. It finally arrived in the 1998 World Cup against Colombia and, of course, it was a trademark free-kick. David swung his left arm backwards and his remarkable right foot forwards. Bang! The ball flew into the bottom corner.

26 MAY 1999, MANCHESTER UNITED 2-1 BAYERN MUNICH

https://www.youtube.com/watch?v=HsCUnTyGJes

In the 1999 Champions League Final, Manchester United had the chance to win a historic Treble. With Roy Keane and Paul Scholes both suspended, David was under even more pressure to deliver. With three minutes to go, they were 1-0 down but thanks to two brilliant corner-kicks from David, United fought back to win 2-1. 'Fergie's Fledglings' just never gave up!

6 OCTOBER 2001, ENGLAND 2-2 GREECE

https://www.youtube.com watch?v=t0GESlaVNdE&t=16s
With seconds to go at Wembley, England were losing
2-1 and their World Cup 2002 dreams were in tatters.
When they won a free-kick, David had one last chance
to save the day for his country. He swung his left arm
backwards and his remarkable right foot forwards.
Bang! The ball flew into the top corner. Thanks to
David, England were off to the World Cup.

10 APRIL 2005, REAL MADRID 4-2 BARCELONA

https://www.youtube.com/watch?v=kYBuXTFOOGg&t=602s
David enjoyed four very happy years as a Galáctico at
Real Madrid. He managed to win the La Liga title, and
this *El Clásico* win against big rivals Barcelona was
probably his Spanish highlight. Although David didn't
get on the scoresheet, he set up goals for Ronaldo and
Michael Owen with his remarkable right foot.

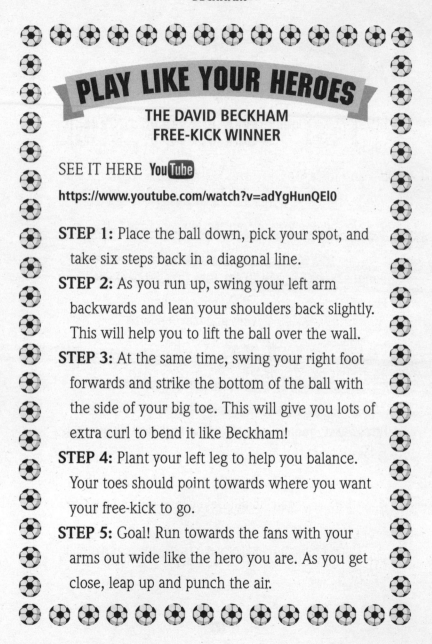

PLAY LIKE YOUR HEROES

THE DAVID BECKHAM
FREE-KICK WINNER

SEE IT HERE You Tube

https://www.youtube.com/watch?v=adYgHunQEI0

STEP 1: Place the ball down, pick your spot, and take six steps back in a diagonal line.

STEP 2: As you run up, swing your left arm backwards and lean your shoulders back slightly. This will help you to lift the ball over the wall.

STEP 3: At the same time, swing your right foot forwards and strike the bottom of the ball with the side of your big toe. This will give you lots of extra curl to bend it like Beckham!

STEP 4: Plant your left leg to help you balance. Your toes should point towards where you want your free-kick to go.

STEP 5: Goal! Run towards the fans with your arms out wide like the hero you are. As you get close, leap up and punch the air.

TEST YOUR KNOWLEDGE

QUESTIONS

1. Which team does David's dad, Ted support?

2. Which team did David's grandad support?

3. What gift did David give to Sir Alex Ferguson when he was 13?

4. Name 3 other members of Manchester United's Class of 92?

5. Which England club did David join on loan in 1995?

6. Which England manager gave David his international debut?

7. Why did David choose the Number 23 shirt at Real Madrid?

8. Who were the other two members of the 'The LA Power Trio'?

9. Who was David's manager at both AC Milan and PSG?

10. How many World Cups did David go to with England?

11. How many World Cup goals did David score?

Answers below. . . No cheating!

1. Manchester United 2. Tottenham 3. A pen, which David later used to sign his first Manchester United contract. 4. Any of the following: Gary Neville, Phil Neville, Nicky Butt, Paul Scholes, Ryan Giggs, John O'Kane, Robbie Savage and Keith Gillespie. 5. Preston North End 6. Glenn Hoddle. 7. Raúl already had the Number 7 shirt and 23 was the number that his basketball hero, Michael Jordan, wore for the Chicago Bulls. 8. Landon Donovan and Robbie Keane 9. Carlo Ancelotti 10. 3 – 1998, 2002 and 2006 11. 3

174

The 2018 World Cup saw your favourite football heroes go head-to head for the ultimate prize – the World Cup.

Complete your collection with six limited-edition international Ultimate Football Heroes.

AVAILABLE NOW

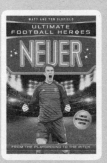

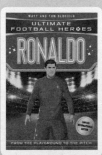

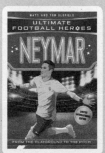

FOLLOW IN THE FOOTSTEPS OF LEGENDS. . .

Bridge the gap between past and present by stepping into the shoes of six classic World Cup heroes and reading their exciting stories – from the playground to the pitch, and to superstardom!

AVAILABLE NOW